# JOURNEY OF THE
# SACRED LEADER

# JOURNEY OF THE SACRED LEADER

✦

## A QUALITATIVE INQUIRY EXAMINING THE COMING OUT PROCESS IN THE ORGANIZATIONAL CULTURE OF A RELIGIOUS SETTING FOR GAY, MALE, PROTESTANT CLERGY

*The Rev. Dr. G. Shane Hibbs*

iUniverse, Inc.
New York  Lincoln  Shanghai

# JOURNEY OF THE SACRED LEADER
## A QUALITATIVE INQUIRY EXAMINING THE COMING OUT PROCESS IN THE ORGANIZATIONAL CULTURE OF A RELIGIOUS SETTING FOR GAY, MALE, PROTESTANT CLERGY

iUniverse books may be ordered through booksellers or by contacting:

iUniverse
2021 Pine Lake Road, Suite 100
Lincoln, NE 68512
www.iuniverse.com
1-800-Authors (1-800-288-4677)

ISBN-13: 978-0-595-40035-5
ISBN-10: 0-595-40035-3

Printed in the United States of America

In our lives, there are brief moments that come and if we are in the right frame of mind, then we know to capture the moment and keep it forever. Several years ago, I had such a moment. I made the move from Ohio to New York and met the most wonderful person in my life. From a day with only change in my pocket to a life that is filled with blessings beyond imagination, I share every day with someone who believes in me, encourages me, and trusts me.

You spent countless hours by yourself as I made this educational journey. You sacrificed and gave unselfishly. You allowed me space and never complained. I can never thank you enough.

You are the greatest part of my life and I could not have made it to this point without your love and support. I love you and dedicate this work to you, my partner, Mark.

# Contents

List of Tables ...................................... *xi*

Abstract ........................................ *xiii*

Chapter 1   INTRODUCTION ................... 1

  Background of the Study ............................ 4

  Statement of the Problem ........................... 5

  Purpose of the Study ............................... 6

  Research Questions ................................ 6

  Nature of the Study ................................ 7

  Significance of the Study ........................... 7

  Definition of Terms ................................ 8

  Assumptions ...................................... 9

  Limitations ...................................... 10

  Organization of the Remainder of the Study ............ 12

Chapter 2   LITERATURE REVIEW .............. 14

  The Coming Out Process ............................ 15

  Clergy Development ............................... 24

  Discrimination .................................... 32

  Organizational Culture: The Church and Homosexuality ..... 38

Chapter 3   METHODOLOGY .................. 51

  Restatement of Purpose ............................ 51

Research Design  . . . . . . . . . . . . . . . . . . . . . . . . . . . . . 52

Target Population . . . . . . . . . . . . . . . . . . . . . . . . . . . . . 55

Selection of Participants  . . . . . . . . . . . . . . . . . . . . . . . . . . . 56

Variables . . . . . . . . . . . . . . . . . . . . . . . . . . . . . . . . . . . 56

Measures . . . . . . . . . . . . . . . . . . . . . . . . . . . . . . . . . . 57

Procedures . . . . . . . . . . . . . . . . . . . . . . . . . . . . . . . . . . 57

Data Collection and Analysis  . . . . . . . . . . . . . . . . . . . . . 59

Expected Findings . . . . . . . . . . . . . . . . . . . . . . . . . . . . 61

Chapter 4    DATA COLLECTION AND
               ANALYSIS . . . . . . . . . . . . . . . . . . . . . . . . 63

Organization of the Results Section . . . . . . . . . . . . . . . . . . . 63

Participant Introductions  . . . . . . . . . . . . . . . . . . . . . . . . 64

The Interviews  . . . . . . . . . . . . . . . . . . . . . . . . . . . . . . 70

Qualitative Analysis of the Text Data  . . . . . . . . . . . . . . . . . 128

Summary  . . . . . . . . . . . . . . . . . . . . . . . . . . . . . . . . . 148

Chapter 5    CONCLUSIONS AND
               RECOMMENDATIONS  . . . . . . . . . . . . . . 151

Discussion . . . . . . . . . . . . . . . . . . . . . . . . . . . . . . . . . 152

Conclusions  . . . . . . . . . . . . . . . . . . . . . . . . . . . . . . . 159

Limitations of the Study . . . . . . . . . . . . . . . . . . . . . . . . . 162

Recommendations for Future Research . . . . . . . . . . . . . . . . 163

*References* . . . . . . . . . . . . . . . . . . . . . . . . . . . . . . . . . *165*

Appendix A:  TELEPHONE SCRIPT TO RECRUIT
               PARTICIPANTS . . . . . . . . . . . . . . . . . . . . 175

Appendix B:  STUDY INFORMATION SHEET . . . . . . . 177

Appendix C:  INFORMED CONSENT FORM . . . . . . . . 179

Appendix D: INTERVIEW QUESTIONS  . . . . . . . . . . 183
Appendix E: INTERVIEW QUESTIONS REVIEW  . . . 185

# List of Tables

Table 1. Stage Theories of Coming Out . . . . . . . . . . . . . . . 18

Table 2. Eysenck Personality Questionnaire Domains . . . . . 26

Table 3. Male Clergy Personality Comparison . . . . . . . . . . 27

Table 4. Participants' Birth and Age . . . . . . . . . . . . . . . . . 70

Table 5. Participants' Age at Coming Out . . . . . . . . . . . . . 75

Table 6. Organizational Culture Responses . . . . . . . . . . . 148

# *Abstract*

This research examines the lived experiences of the coming out process for gay, male, Protestant clergy in a religious organizational culture, as well as the reported responses attributed to the members of the religious organizational culture. Research has presented religious culture in a pejorative view. Autobiographical writings of individual clergy recount the experience as traumatic and transforming. While research exists on the coming out process and gays in the church, there is no current empirical research that examines the leaders and their coming out experience with such an organizational culture. Eight gay, male, Protestant clergy, either known to the researcher as an openly gay minister in the community or referred to the researcher, are interviewed utilizing a standardized open-ended interview process. The participants are selected through purposeful sampling to gain a diversity of participants. The interview transcripts are then processed by the researcher employing the Heuristic model of research. The researcher identifies themes and categories that exist in the data gathered from all participants. After these themes and categories were identified, they were interpreted in terms which examine how the coming out process is affected by the religious organizational culture and how the religious organizational culture responds to the participant's experience. It is expected that the results will shed important light on how religious organizational culture responds to gay, male, Protestant clergy in their process of coming out.

# *Acknowledgments*

Every successful journey is never made alone. There are those who assist, those who inspire, and those who accommodate. The journey of my doctoral degree and the task of my dissertation are no different. I would like to thank those people who were my support on this journey.

I would like to first and foremost thank my mentor and chair, Dr. Wayland Secrest. This journey would not have been possible without you. You were my guide and a voice of wisdom along the way. Thank you for all those nights of long distance phone calls, my overabundance of emails, and frantic panics along the way. When I began this journey, I spoke to you about whether I could make it or not. You believed in me and I have finally made it. Thank you so much.

To my committee, Dr. Donna DiMatteo and Dr. Paul Maione, I would like to thank you for your countless hours of reading, re-reading, and the constant barrage of emails sent your way.

This study would not have been possible without each and every one of the willing participants who opened their lives to me in this research. Thank you so much for making yourself vulnerable. Your lives are inspiration for all of us on our journey.

To Dr. Theresa Pavone, I would like to thank you for being my set of extra eyes as you served as an independent reviewer of my paper.

I would like to thank Dr. Gilbert Tippy for his countless hours of reading drafts, making edits, listening to a frustrated doctoral student and allowing me space to grow. You have been an inspiration.

I would like to thank Dr. William Knack for your encouragement along the way.

I would like to give a special thanks to Blanca Schneider, Marleene Bhan, and Treesa Varghese. These three people (my co-workers) have done more than anyone can imagine. You were my friends through times when I was often absent as I was engulfed in the doctoral process.

I would like to thank Rev. Paul B. Milholland and Rev. Hank Lay. You carried the weight of my church, helped keep everything together around me, and spent time keeping me focused while I traveled this journey. Your help and assistance is much appreciated.

I would like to thank Mr. Westley R. Villazon and Mrs. Helen B. Villazon. Before I started this journey, your words of kindness, assistance, and accommodations were more than I could ever ask from any person. You are like a second set of parents. I can never thank you enough.

I would like to thank Ms. Darlene Hopkins. You were my friend and confidante. You spent many nights telling me never to give up, never surrender, and never to take no. You believed in me throughout the years. You inspired me with your persistence and tenacity. You are a person to look up to and to strive to be like. You are my hero.

I would like to thank my parents Steven and Donna Eaglin and Gary and Dee Hibbs for always encouraging me to believe that I can achieve anything that I want to. You started me on this journey and for that I can never thank you enough.

I would like to thank Long Island Community Fellowship, my church. You took the year in stride as my focus was on completing this research. You never complained and you always allowed me my space. You truly are the reason I keep going.

# 1

# *INTRODUCTION*

*The young man was sitting there on the side of the plush grassy hill in his splendor as a king on the side of a mountain. Was it the grass that caressed his body or simply the sun stroking his face that gave the strong sense of numbness? He looked out as he saw all his colleagues leaving for lunch. Unlike a prince or a king, he was not looking about a kingdom but instead his head had fallen in defeat.*

*The day had been long, but it was barely past noon. The last car was pulling away leaving him alone on the firing range. The cadets and instructors had all gone to lunch. The events leading to this day* not only could be remembered but could never be forgotten. Everyday it was the same thing. It was waking up as his spirit went lower and lower. It was opening his eyes, as his life grew darker. It was simply the unconscious act of breathing that required him to make a conscious decision to do so.

As everyone left, the loneliness sunk in. They weren't his friends anyway. He was alone in life. That was the problem. He was always alone. He would wake up, go through the day, and finally fall asleep…all alone. He hadn't talked to his family in some time and there seemed to be no relationship there worth maintaining. At 25 years of age, the lonely soul, who was but a child in his heart, had lost everything. Now things would surely change.

He had been thinking of suicide for the past year. As more and more of his life slipped into what seemed to be a chaotic tidal wave that was out of control he was grasping and clinging to every moment so it would not join the rapidly moving life that was out of control. It stole more and more of him until there was not much left.

Love is what keeps our heart alive. The young man felt the coldness in his heart as he realized there was no one to love him. Faith is what inspires us to believe. Everything he believed in had failed him. There was no faith left. Hope is what encourages us to keep going in spite of obstacles. Finally, there was no hope left in sight but everyday was filled with plenty of obstacles. He had lost the most basic elements to survive: faith, hope and love.

The young man pulled out his weapon from its holster. The cold steel barrel of the 9mm Smith and Wesson glistened in the sun. He pulled out a new clip that contained three bullets. The ammunition was ready and the time had come. His hands began to shake uncontrollably. As the clip seemed to increase exponentially in weight and it bobbed from side to side as he attempted to insert it, finally he was able to make its way into the gun. He chambered the weapon and listened as the bullet fell into place so it was ready to fire. The hammer was cocked back and the slight pull of the trigger is what was needed.

He placed the gun up to the temple of his head. Thoughts started racing through his mind as he placed a finger on the trigger. He was a trained marksman and began to think about the situation more clearly. There might be a jerk reaction from the kick of the gun as it fired. Putting the gun to the temple might not be right. This was the last chance for peace. his was his only hope. He couldn't screw this up.

*He dropped the weapon to his mouth. He opened up as he stuck the weapon in and angled the barrel to ensure the discharge of the bullet goes directly into the brain. This was it. This was the last effort that was being reached for to gain peace.*

G. S. H., Case Notes

The case study above is one example of a minister's attempting to integrate the self identity of a gay male with a religious organizational culture. While this individual is failing in his pursuit of making a successful assimilation, there is an attempt to regain control of the identity development process that occurs for many gay men and lesbians when they are required to interact with a religious corporate culture. Out of over 2,500 Christian denominations in America there are very few that accept gay males and lesbians (Sherkat, 2002). This creates a challenge to reconcile the coming out process with a religious organizational culture that claims to have a heavenly foundation. The minister who finds himself between the development of his personal identity and this organizational cultural identity may find himself in a conundrum.

The case study may not be a common representation of what happens when an individual is left to balance an organizational culture that may not be as supportive as others with a developing sexual orientation identity; however, this case study provides an insight as to the depth of despair that may be examined in this research. Individuals dedicate their life to an organization (The Church), only to find themselves in the challenge of choosing between an organizational culture that is "given from above" or to be themselves. It is one thing for this to impact members of a church; however, the clergy are the very leaders who are charged with the responsibility of emulating the organizational culture as a whole. This is a phenomenon that occurs between the individual in their role as minister and the conflicting identity of self. This study seeks to explore the religious organizational culture that is being balanced in the lives of religious leaders who are experiencing the coming out process.

# Background of the Study

There are several social and political issues that come to the forefront in developing societies. Currently, homosexuality and the church is a hot topic of conversation in the current American culture. The Evangelical Lutheran Church (2005) is currently conducting studies on sexuality to assist in making a determination on such topics as the blessing of same sex marriages and the ordination of openly and practicing gays and lesbians. Evangelical Lutheran Church officials are not alone in this question. The United Churches of Christ are currently dealing with a ban on their national advertising because of the inclusion of gays and lesbians, while other religious organizations are being allowed to continue with their marketing campaigns (Guess, 2005). While issues pertinent to gay and lesbian rights and supportive development are ever pressing in today's media and culture, gay men and lesbians have been navigating this gap psychologically for their entire life.

Van Loon (2003) explored what it meant for Evangelical Christians to deal with sexual identities that were not in agreement with the faith and beliefs of their communities. However, the research stops short of examining the leaders in their coming out process. There are individuals who identify themselves as Christian who are dealing with coming out; however, what happens when those persons who are coming out are the guardians, elders, and leaders of the very faith that condemns who they are?

Coleman (1982) explained that when a person is coming out, the acceptance or rejection of sexuality, from individuals whose relationship is valued, is extremely critical to the identity development of the individual. Acceptance from others allows the individual to come to terms with sexuality and the individual will be able to dismiss the myths and stereotypes that have surrounded the pre-coming out stage. The individual who experiences rejection will experience an affirmation of the pejorative myths and stereotypes that were present in the pre-coming out stage leading to an internalized homophobia.

Coleman explained that rejection can cause the individual to conceal their identity for years to come and provides a chronic low-grade depression and extremely low self image.

Ordained clergy who are faced with the developmental cycle of coming out are not only dealing with a personal crisis; however, they must deal with an organizational crisis as they attempt to reconcile an organizational culture that may be unsupportive or even hostile with their very identity as a person and a leader. Researchers are beginning to look at the development of gay Christians and gay Churches (Lukenbill, 1998; Perry & Swicegood, 1990; Sherkat, 2002; Yip, 2003). It is acknowledged by most researchers that the Church produces an un-affirming culture to come out in. One of the dynamics that is left for the research community to examine is to look at the leaders who are experiencing this phenomenon of a religious organizational culture. The individuals that often times get left out of the research are the very ones who have to navigate the merger of their organizational culture (i.e., their faith, their vocation) and the developmental process of coming out—ministers. This study attempts to address that void in research.

## Statement of the Problem

This study examines the phenomenon of the coming out process of gay male clergy while integrating a religious organizational culture. Van Loon (2003) explained that this is a clashing issue for a lay member of a congregation that may often lead to suicide, and still yet, the very leaders that must navigate this phenomenon are given the ultimate decision of creating the paradoxical equilibrium between the organizational culture and their sexual identity. This study examines gay, male, Protestant clergy and identifies themes that emerge from their experiences as they reflect on living this experience.

# Purpose of the Study

The purpose of this study is to provide a heuristic inquiry to gain a generalized understanding of how gay, male, Protestant clergy perceive the organizational culture of the church on their coming out process and how they travel around the obstacles that may exist in such an environment during this experience. While there are several studies providing insight to the coming out process and gay Christians (Cass, 1984; Coleman, 1982; Lukenbill, 1998; Newman & Muzzonigro, 1993; Perry & Swicegood, 1990; Sherkat, 2002; Troiden, 1989; Van Loon, 2003; Yip, 2003), the very leaders of these organizations are given a mandate to present a sense of identity that reflects the religious organizational culture. They are set apart and given the responsibility of reflecting the values, morals, and generalized culture of their organization. They must navigate the coming out process while under the scrutiny of congregations and denominational officials. There are no current studies known to this author that examine such a phenomenon.

# Research Questions

This research project answers several questions. What is the impact of the lived experience of the coming out process for gay, male, Protestant clergy in religious organizational cultures? Is the organizational culture supportive or nonsupportive? How does the level of support of the church affect an individual's experience of the stages of the coming out process? How do the individuals reconcile their belief structure as taught by the organizational culture in which they are immersed with their own developmental cycle of coming out? What is the individual leader's reaction and interaction with the organizational culture during and after this process?

# Nature of the Study

This study implements the heuristic model of research methodology, while endeavoring to construct a life history or a portrait of the participants as they attempt to navigate this phenomenon.

# Significance of the Study

The development cycle for individuals includes the formation of an identity. The healthy identity formation of the homosexual male in the coming out process is directly correlated with whether there is a positive acceptance of the alternative sexual orientation or it is avidly objected to (Coleman, 1982). If the person is rejected by close family or friends and this has a significant impact, then how much greater would the impact of being rejected by what is perceived to be a superior being, a God.

Coleman (1982) explained that the more value placed on a colleague, friend, or family member then the more destructive or constructive their view of the sexual identity development will have on the person. What happens when the identified party that disagrees seems to be a God with whom the minister claims to have a relationship? The impact could be devastating.

The Rev. Elder Nancy Wilson, the current presiding officer over the Metropolitan Community Churches, estimates that there are tens of thousands of clergy individuals who are dealing with the coming out process in the United States (personal communication, March 4, 2005). Therefore, with estimates that place gay clergy in the thousands, it becomes essential to address the development of such a culture.

This study attempts to understand how individuals deal with the process of the coming out process in a religious environment, which has been recorded as not necessarily being supportive, and how it is perceived by the individual experiencing this phenomenon. Furthermore, it is a goal of this study to examine how the individual interacts with the religious organizational culture, while studies would claim this is a nonsupportive environment.

# Definition of Terms

*Calling.* Calling is the religious concept of a vocation coming from outside one's own choice. The cultural implication is the external, God, choosing the individual to do such a work rather than the individual choosing the work. It is important for the readers of this study to have an understanding of how the cultural view of vocation, calling, can impact those who are following after a clergy tract.

*Coming out.* Coleman (1982) defined the coming out process as the acknowledgement of one's same-sex interest to oneself and one's public. Newman and Muzzonigro (1993) defined the coming out process as the development of a gay or lesbian identity. Floyd and Stein (2002) described the coming out process as an identity formation process that is unique to individuals who are gay, lesbians, and bisexuals. The definition that will be utilized in this research is that coming out is the process of recognizing, accepting, and communicating one's sexual orientation to oneself and others for gay, lesbian, and bisexual individuals.

*Heuristic.* This research focuses on the lived experience of these individuals, of which the author is a part. This necessitates that the research to be conducted in a heuristic model. Heuristic inquiry seeks to identify what the meaning of a lived experience is (Moustakas, 1990). Heuristics does not attempt to objectify the phenomenon; however, it attempts to be true to the people who are living the aforesaid phenomenon. It is understanding the phenomenon through empathy.

*Organizational culture.* Organizational culture, sometimes referred to as corporate culture, is the essence of what is acceptable and unacceptable behavior in the context of the organization itself. It is how the morality is defined, the beliefs are developed, and the behavior played out. Schermerhorn, Hunt, and Osborn explained that organizational culture is "the system of shared actions, values, and beliefs that develops within an organization and guides the behavior of its members" (2000, p. G-8). Molenaar, Brown, Caile, and Smith (2002) defined organizational culture as the beliefs, values and behaviors that are shared by all members in a company. One can clearly see the pattern of the anthropological focus of these definitions. Waters (2004) defined organizational culture as "the source of motivated and coordinated activities within organizations, activities that serve as a foundation for practices and behaviors that endure…" (p.36). This research will use a definition which integrates each of these definitions. What an individual can see, experience, and live in a given organization that is in common with all the other individuals who are in that same organization is how organizational culture is created, defined, and transmitted. For the purposes of this paper, organizational culture will be defined as the shared belief structures of an organization that defines behaviors and attitudes.

*Vocation.* For the purposes of this paper, a vocation is defined as a career path which is chosen by an individual, which includes their strategies for advancement and development into the field as a whole.

## Assumptions

The researcher assumes there is a relationship between the impact of the religious culture and the coming out process. Coleman (1982) explained the closer the individual is to the person coming out, the greater the impact. The researcher assumes the participants of this study have dealt with the coming out process and place a significant relationship with their religious culture. A significant relationship is being evaluated by examining whether the clergy are remaining active in the church, whether as a lay attendee or continuing to be active clergy. In order to dedicate one's life to such a vocation then it is assumed there is a great deal of connection.

Another assumption this researcher makes is that a sample size of eight persons will provide the researcher a sufficient sample to begin understanding the phenomenon in question. The heuristic evaluation of eight persons will be the basis for the development of categories and themes. Eight persons' experiences will be evaluated to determine these dynamics that exist.

The researcher assumes that the coming out process can be described through a phase/stage theory. One can break down the actual coming out process into groupings of similar behaviors which are categorized into stages. This author assumes the best way to describe the coming out process is through the stage theories put forth in the literature review of this research (Cass, 1984; Coleman, 1982; Newman & Muzzonigro, 1993; Troiden, 1989).

# Limitations

Every study has limitations. While some may view certain qualities as limitations, others will view them as the very strength of a study. Qualitative research is discovery oriented research and therefore does not claim to provide quantitative insight. Therefore, the goal of this study is discovery, not generalizability. The lack of this quality may be perceived as a limitation; however, it is the very strength and what mandates this type of research be conducted.

Another limitation the research may present is the proximity of the researcher to the topic area. This research acknowledges that being part of the demographic being studied may influence the outcomes; however, precautions are being taken to attempt to make the results of this research verifiable. Some of these steps include the utilization of individuals to review questions for appropriateness, wording, and order; having another colleague read over the material to determine if the same themes and categories come through; and, the research is inserting an epoche stage to reduce any undo influence on the research direction. Each of these steps is addressed in greater detail in chapter 3.

Quantitative readers may find its limitations steeped in focus, demographic of sample, hermeneutic of suspicion, and its lack of generalizability. This study does not claim any of these qualities; however, each is explored a bit further. As previously stated, this research is a process of discovery.

One may perceive a limitation of this study is that it is narrowly focused on gay, male, Protestant clergy. In order to make the research manageable it is essential to narrow the field of focus. This is one of the strengths of the qualitative design.

Another limitation is that the sample of the study is limited to the regional demographics of the North East. While the participants in this study come from a variety of places throughout the United States, they currently all reside in the North East. This limitation comes from the availability of the researcher to gain access to the participants.

Since the study is a heuristic study then it can be argued that it lacks generalizability, objectivity, and may have a hermeneutic of suspicion. In a lecture, Dr. Kim Kostere (2004) paralleled the heuristic process, if done well, to that of poetry. It is a relationship with the material. It is the interaction of the researcher and the subject.

Hibbs (2003) explained that in any relationship what we love most about a person is what we will hate the most. The unique focus that is provided by reaching to the meaning of a specific phenomenon does not attempt to provide a quality of generalizability. The author's perspective which provides unique insight also provides a proximal issue in discovery, which was previously addressed.

Cohen and Swerdlik (1999) explained that generalizability is to have an instrument or research have the ability to be applied to other groups in similar settings. Heuristics is examining the lived experiences of specific participants. All individuals' life experiences change. No two people will have the same experience and even the same participants may reflect and provide a different lived experience after a period of time has passed. There is limited generalizability in the heuristic model.

McDonald (2001) explained that heuristics understands the impossibility of being neutral and therefore makes no such claim.

One of the claims against the heuristic inquiry process is the lack of objectivity. The author is so immersed in the topic, writing from their own perspective, that it becomes difficult for objective truth to surface. Heuristics allows the author to immerse oneself and become part of the research. The argument against the heuristic inquiry is that once an author has violated the boundaries between researcher and subject, how can true objective research be conducted? While conducting this research, the author of this paper came across the term hermeneutic of suspicion when speaking with a colleague. The hermeneutic of suspicion simply says that when a researcher is coming from a lived experience oneself, then how does the reader know if the research is not simply part of an agenda the researcher wishes to achieve. As previously stated, steps are being taken to insure the verifiability of the research.

How do we know this researcher did not have an agenda? The questioning of the validity becomes very easy when the researcher does not disclose information. It is essential for the heuristic research to provide all the data and validation. Even yet, the research will be questioned if it is putting the agenda of the researcher forward. In order to deal with such a possibility, this author has included a process to deal with such an agenda (see chapter 3).

## Organization of the Remainder of the Study

The remaining chapters include a literature review, methodology, results, and discussion. The literature review contains a review of the coming out process, clergy development, discrimination, and organizational culture. This provides the reader an introduction to the foundations of research which this study is based upon.

The next chapter, methodology, includes how the heuristic model is utilized to conduct this study. This section will discuss how many participants will be utilized, the method of data collection, and data interpretation. The exact steps and actions of the researcher are documented.

Then, a chapter on the results is presented. This is the data that were gathered in the interview and journaling process. This is where a synthesis of the data is shown. The themes and portraits that occur are presented for the reader.

Finally, what does all this mean? The final section will include a discussion of the results and implications for further research. This section is vital to the synthesis of the data as it actually discusses the implications for the research that was conducted and how it can be utilized. It is the interaction between the results and the literature review and the implications that come from them.

# 2

# *LITERATURE REVIEW*

Research has previously been conducted on various topics that impact the design and findings of this study. It becomes necessary to review that literature so the reader may better understand the direction and design of the study. The following is a review of literature on various topics that influence this study. The topics reviewed are the coming out process, clergy development, discrimination, and organizational culture.

The coming out process is reviewed and information presented on the concepts of stage theory. Developmental constructs and various researchers' presentations are presented. This paper puts forth Coleman's (1982) model as the framework whereby this information is presented.

The next review is of research on clergy development. Clergy development is divided into three discussions: clergy personality and selection, training/credentialing of clergy, and clergy effectiveness. This information provides a snapshot of what current research is being conducted with clergy and their vocations.

Discrimination is the third area of literature review provided. An introduction is provided as the foundation for understanding the discrimination process. It is elaborated with three elements: stereotyping, prejudice, and discrimination. This is followed by how discrimination occurs within an organizational culture. Gays and lesbians have a unique dynamic whereby they must make a choice to reveal their sexual orientation henceforth placing themselves in a position to be discriminated against in an organizational culture.

Finally, organizational culture is discussed. A brief overview is provided to allow the reader to understand what an organizational culture is. This is followed by a review of the research on organizational cultures of religious organizations.

# The Coming Out Process

Coming out seems to affect different persons in a variety of ways. Factors such as age, social support structure and social economic status affect the process (Beaty, 1999; Coleman, 1982; Dube, 2000; Floyd & Stein, 2002; McFarland & McMahon, 1999; Newman & Muzzonigro, 1993). In order to gain an understanding of the development cycle for gays, lesbians, and bisexuals it is imperative to understand the developmental cycle of the coming out process.

Dube (2000) conducted a study with 166 gay or bisexual males between the ages of 16 and 39. Participants were asked to give the age at which they experienced each milestone of sexual development. Based upon this study, Dube claims this development is identity centered for younger individuals and sex centered for older individuals. Dube explains this phenomenon exists because older males have a higher level of internalized homophobia. According to this study, it is more likely for the older individuals dealing with sexual orientation to have heterosexual identities developed with hidden homosexual identities.

Newman and Muzzonigro (1993) concluded a stage model of coming out is appropriate for gay male adolescents. Twenty-seven gay male youth between the ages of 17 and 20 participated in a study filling out questionnaires exploring the conceptualization of the stage model. While the conclusion of the coming out process being explained in respect of the stage models is limited to gay male adolescents, other research supports the theory of the stage model applying to the coming out process being generalized.

Cass (1984) explained the theory of developmental stages in the coming out process has little empirical support. Cass explains the movement from the construct of viewing homosexuality as pathology to the construct of a developmental stage model is where the study of homosexuality is currently. Cass questions the reliability and validity of the stage model. Cass conducted research on the validity of a six-stage model she proposed.

Furthermore, Newman and Muzzonigro (1993) reported a majority of male adolescents acknowledging a crush on another male adolescent by the age of 12. Floyd and Stein (2002) placed the average age of the crush by the age of 9. This acknowledges an early identity beginning to develop; however, the stages may be repressed or arrested.

McFarland and McMahon (1999) explained that the typical male moves from boy psychology to man psychology when humiliation and limitations are realized. If this is entered too early it robs the adolescent of their youth. This occurs when the youth experiences the possibility of humiliation for being different. Floyd and Stein (2002) expanded on this by explaining that while the individuals who acknowledge and accept sexual orientation earlier in life have a greater probability of having a positive and healthy identity, they have a greater possibility to experience humiliation earlier which leads to a higher risk of suicide.

In order to examine the research further, it becomes necessary to provide some structure to the discussion. This will be accomplished by utilizing a stage model. There are several models which explain the stages of coming out (see Table 1). Troiden (1989) utilized a four-stage model that includes: sensitization, identity confusion, identity assumption, and commitment. Cass (1984) proposed a six-stage model that includes: identity confusion, identity comparison, identity tolerance, identity acceptance, identity pride, and identity synthesis. Coleman (1982) utilized a five-stage model which includes: pre-coming out, coming out, exploration, first relationships, and integration. No matter how you package the psychological phenomena of coming out, it appears the stages are very similar. For the purpose of this study, Coleman (1982) will be utilized in order to provide a structure. Coleman provides appropriate depth and is a median between the alternate four- and six-stage processes.

Coleman (1982) listed the five stages of coming out: pre-coming out, coming out, exploration, first relationships, and integration. As Coleman explained, these stages do not occur consecutively or without problems. Instead, an individual can go from one stage to the next and for others a stage may become arrested causing the individual to experience developmental, psychological, and social difficulties.

### Stage 1: Pre-Coming Out

This stage refers to a preawareness to the very initial stages of awareness of one's sexuality. Newman and Muzzonigro (1993) reported the primary description in this stage is confusion. Individuals are not sure what is happening. There are feelings of confusion, denial, guilt, and shame.

**Table 1. Stage Theories of Coming Out**

| Troiden (1989) | Cass (1984) | Coleman (1982) |
|---|---|---|
| Sensitization (an awareness that the individual is different, sexually attracted to the same sex) | Identity confusion (the questioning of current heterosexual identity occurs) | Pre-Coming out (an initial awareness of same sex attraction occurs that are often dismissed) |
| Identity confusion (the thoughts that he/she may be gay are coupled with not accepting it) | Identity comparison (an initial acceptance occurs as the comparisons between the former identity and current identity occurs) | Coming out (the self-admission occurs where the individual acknowledges their own homosexuality) |
| Identity assumption (the individual accepts they are gay and begins to interact with other gay persons) | Identity tolerance (accepting the new identity, the individual begins to seek out exposure to the culture of the new identity) | Exploration (process of experimenting and testing the new culture of the gay identity) |
| Commitment (previous gay thoughts and interaction are turned into action where the person begins to interact comfortably with the gay culture) | Identity acceptance (contact with the gay culture promotes a positive view of the new gay self) | First relationships (the individual is able to see themselves as able to love and be loved and enter into the first gay relationship) |
|  | Identity pride (the individual identifies with gay cultures and begins to devalue heterosexual culture) | Integration (the individual is able to integrate the value of self and normal development to continue in the life cycle) |

**Table 1. Stage Theories of Coming Out (Continued)**

| Troiden (1989) | Cass (1984) | Coleman (1982) |
| --- | --- | --- |
| | Identity synthesis (the splitting of good homosexual culture and bad heterosexual culture moves to a combined understanding and acceptance and valuing of both cultures) | |

Coleman (1982) explained that while contemporary society is more tolerant of the coming out process it is still considered deviant, sick, or immoral by many. Corrigan and Matthews (2003) explained that being homosexual carries a stigma that requires someone to deal with an additional process of development entitled coming out.

The pre-coming out stage is where internalized homophobia sets in for many individuals. Internalized homophobia is when the individual applies the societal stereotypes to oneself. This creates a very negative self-image. Coleman (1982) explained that the individual will begin to see themselves as society sees them.

The negative self-image is perpetuated as the individual hears friends, family, and colleagues make negative statements about homosexuals and homosexuality. Coleman (1982) explained these statements of rejection are often over-generalized so the individual doesn't like anything about themselves. This overgeneralization extends to areas of their life that have nothing to do with sexuality.

Coleman (1982) claimed the individual, in response to this rejection and overgeneralization, conceals their overall identity. Individuals in this stage will not reveal their identity to anyone including a therapist. The rejection causes a conforming acceptable sexual behavior while an internal struggle will remain ever present.

Beaty (1999) explained that a family's ability or inability to unconditionally accept, love and care for a member of the family will lend to the individual's identity development. Whether the individual is gay or lesbian, it is important to have a supportive environment. Beaty claims there is a lack of research to conclude too much from the coming out process; however, he points out the familial support impacts youth. This is only compounded when undergoing such a process as coming out.

### Stage 2: Coming Out

The coming out stage is when the individual stops fighting the notion of a different sexual identity (Coleman, 1982). Coleman explained this does not mean they consider themselves gay or lesbian. They simply stop dismissing the notion and begin a process of reconciliation and making peace with themselves and their sexuality.

The acceptance or rejection of sexuality at this point is extremely critical to the identity development of the individual (Coleman, 1982). Acceptance from others can allow the individual to come to terms with sexuality and the individual will be able to dismiss the mythology that surrounded the pre-coming out stage. It is the affirmation which will lead to allowing the individual to openly discuss and disclose to others. Rejection experienced in this stage is a powerful setback to the identity development of the individual. The individual who experiences rejection will experience an affirmation of the internalized negative homophobia that was present in the pre-coming out stage. Coleman explained that rejection can cause the individual to conceal their identity for years to come and provides a chronic low-grade depression and extremely low self image.

Floyd and Stein (2002) explained that if positive experiences have occurred for the individual coming out, then this stage occurs more smoothly. This lends itself to positive self image development. Coleman (1982) explained the closer the relationship of the person disclosed to the more powerful the affirmation effect is on the individual who is disclosing. It is affirmational to disclose to a close friend. It is even more powerful when a positive disclosure occurs to a parent or close family member. The more significant the person is to the individual the greater the positive effect.

This works on the converse, as well. If rejection occurs from someone close, the greater the damage will be. The more significant the person is to the individual the greater the negative effect that will occur.

This stage is crucial in identity formation for a homosexual. Marszalek and Cashwell (1999) explained that individuals who experience a positive and affirming reception from others, including therapist, have a much better probability of developing a positive sense of self. A good or bad self image hangs in the balance.

## Stage 3: Exploration

The Exploration stage refers to the exploring and experimenting with a new identity (Coleman, 1982). This is a period of firsts. Coleman explained this stage is social exploration, as well as sexual exploration. Therefore, it is common for this stage to include the first contact with gay/lesbian culture. It is the first outing to the gay/lesbian bar and picking up the gay/lesbian newspaper. It is the first time the individual is seeking out others like themselves.

It is important to understand that heterosexual sexual development typically occurs throughout the adolescent years and the exploration of the homosexual sexual development may be occurring in an individual's 30s, 40s, and 50s (Coleman, 1982). This causes a misconception of promiscuity and immaturity to be ascribed in this stage. The exploring is an exploration of an identity they have not fully known.

Dube (2000) explained that according to models, such as Coleman, sexual behavior is a key aspect in developing an understanding and identification as a homosexual. It is a confirmation of what they may have believed to be true. Dube pointed out the limitation of this is the individuals who pursue sexual acts before dealing with the acceptance issue. Coleman would reply by reiterating the lack of sequential congruity does not dismiss the conceptualization of these stages. As previously stated, the stages do not necessarily occur consecutively to one another.

The exploration stage may include the sexual exploration; however, it is more about exploring the new identity that is being discovered to be their own. Cass (1984) characterized this phase by calling it identity evaluation, group identification, and social interaction. Cass explains the identity evaluation is the degree of acceptance of the self and the negative stereotypes associated with that identity of the self. Group identification manifests itself when an individual is able to identify with a group in society (i.e., homosexuals). Social interaction refers to the contact with others with the same identity (i.e., gay bars, gay clubs, and gay bookstores). Sexual exploration is one piece of the identity exploration that is occurring; however, the exploration stage refers to a much more in-depth cultural experience.

There is a part of the individual they don't know themselves. Therefore, this stage is the exploration of society and sexuality in response to their new identity. A sense of acceptance, interpersonal skills, and personal attractiveness develops during the exploration stage (Coleman, 1982).

### Stage 4: First Relationships

First relationship stage is when the individual finds themselves worthy of love and begins openly to seek the stability of a relationship (Coleman, 1982). Hibbs (2003) said that most individuals move into this phase in life and spend a life time seeking that special someone to love them. Hibbs went on to explain that when an individual accepts themselves enough to love themselves they will desire the love and affection of another. The desire to build a relationship (family) will occur.

The contact of first relationships can be devastating to the individual. The disenfranchisement of relationships not working will bring the person to questioning if relationships can ever work (Hibbs, 2003). Hibbs explained that the myths and pitfalls of relationships can cause an individual to believe that the fantasy in the mind can never come true. Is there really someone out there for me or not? This stage of relationships brings the gay, lesbian or bisexual individual to a similar stage with everyone else. Individuals, whether homosexual, bisexual or heterosexual, go through a stage of first relationships.

Dube (2000) pointed out that most romantic and sexual relationships among same sex couples in this stage are kept very secretive. The implications an individual carries from society will stigmatize the relationship causing the individual to be very cautious before releasing the information that they are involved in a relationship. This is just another example of the individual hiding parts of their identity.

This stage will see the individual continue in one destructive relationship after another or the individual will assimilate the learning and the relationships will evolve into healthy relationships (Coleman, 1982). Healthy relationships occur as part of a developmental and maturation process. Coleman went on further to say that identity development, although maybe delayed, is still forming at this stage.

### Stage 5: Integration

The integration stage is when the individual can integrate their sexual orientation identity into their overall person. This integration of identity is a process that is long and painful. At this stage, the individual will then progress through adulthood and the remaining development. The major factor is to understand that while this is finally a healthy place to be, it can take a lifetime to get here.

Individuals in the integration stage are all different ages. They are in their 20s, 30s, 40s, 50s, and some even older. This brings a whole new perspective to adulthood and the remaining development that will occur.

Groves and Ventura (1983) explained once individuals can accept one's identity as a homosexual, there is a decrease of stress and anxiety in their life. Groves and Ventura specifically researched women; however, this could be generalized quite easily to both male and female homosexuals. Once the individual can integrate their sexuality into their identity, there is a release of the stress and anxiety of hiding themselves. Integration is easier said than done. It does require a life time of work as one attempts to achieve the integration of who they are with the self.

### Coming Out Summary

The studies reported here show a clear influential connection to the persons and groups of persons that surround an individual during the coming out process. There is also a clear and distinct increase in stress levels and anxiety producing experiences. Individuals experience an increased awareness of who they are coupled with the confusion of understanding their self. This is a period of time which yields many difficulties.

This process of coming out occurs in several stages. Research proposes different theories of the developmental stage theory. This research will rely on Coleman (1982) for a five-stage model.

# Clergy Development

In order to assist the understanding of clergy, it is important to understand the research that revolves around clergy development. There are three primary areas of research surrounding the construct of clergy development: clergy personality and selection, training/credentialing of clergy, and clergy effectiveness. Each of these three topics is reviewed in this section.

This researcher must offer a caveat to the reader in respect to the level of peer-reviewed psychological research in this field. While there is a plethora of information provided on the three topics aforementioned, there is very little empirical research. The preponderance of the research is presented by sources that have limited reliability. Therefore, the material from nonempirical sources is not presented. There is significant research to contribute without the need of implementing nonempirical sources.

## Clergy Personality

Research on clergy personality is not new. Denominations have attempted to determine factors that may serve as a predictor for effective clergy and henceforth began by studying personality traits of current clergy. Clergy personality refers to traits and characteristics of a minister that are found to be in common with others. Most research is denominational specific.

Kennedy, Heckler, Kobler, and Walker (1977) conducted early research on the personality of ministers utilizing Roman Catholic priests. The conclusion of their work is that priests often have an underdeveloped sense of identity. This is primarily attributed to their identity is more related to the priesthood than to the self. Kennedy et al. concluded that priest are influenced by the expectation of others and their sense of security that is drawn from their vocational aspirations.

Robbins, Francis, Haley, and Kay (2001) utilized the Revised Eysenck Personality Questionnaire which utilizes three domains: extraversion, neuroticism, and psychoticism (see Table 2). The questionnaire includes a lie scale, also. Robbins et al. explained distinct differences that occur on the psychoticism and neuroticism scales. The research of Robbins et al. was conducted with male Methodist ministers in England.

The Robbins et al. (2001) research assessed 1,339 Methodist ministers in England. The research shows lower neuroticism and psychoticism scale scores and a higher extraversion score (see Table 3). This differentiated not simply from the male norm; however, the differences in the scores were compared to female norms, as well.

Research shows that ministry appeals to males that are more likely to show traditionally feminine characteristics such as tender-minded and gentleness (Robbins et al., 2001). Robbins et al. explained that extraversion, sensitive, caring, and stable personalities, as depicted by the Eysenck's model, are often more common feminine characteristics; however, these are often the characteristics of male ministers.

Thereby, Robbins et al. concluded that male ministers are more feminine than the traditional male.

### Table 2. Eysenck Personality Questionnaire Domains

| Domain | Operational Explanation |
|---|---|
| Neuroticism | Domain is an indicator of the ability to stably react (lower scores) vs. those who react out of proportion (higher scores). |
| Psychoticism | Domain is an indicator of the ability to care and show empathy (high scores) vs. those who react more insensitive or cold (lower scores). |
| Extraversion | Domain is an indicator of individuals who are introverted (lower scores) vs. those who enjoy being around people and who are more sociable (higher scores). |

Francis and Pearson (1990) administered the Eysenck Personality Questionnaire to 40 Anglican ministers in England during a midcareer consultation. Francis and Pearson preceded Robbins et al. (2001), and provided the premise for Robbins et al. to conduct the further study. Francis and Pearson find that while the psychoticism scale may be in common with the Methodist ministers that there is a higher level of neuroticism. In this study the authors do not provide many conclusions; however, they simply conclude that more research should be completed. This construct is supported by research conducted among Episcopal clergy (Robbins, Francis, & Rutledge, 1997). Anglican (Episcopal) ministers were found to score lower on the psychoticism scale which implies similar tender-mindedness characteristics. This research implies the nurturing and caring nature one may assume to find in a minister. Robbins et al. bring conclusions more in line with the Methodist Study.

Evangelical clergy differ from Robbins et al. research model in respect to the neuroticism scale. While Robbins et al. places a lower level of neuroticism than the traditional male norm, the evangelical clergy have a higher level of neuroticism which is more common with the traditional male (Francis, 2002). This is consistent with the emotional detachment.

### Table 3. Male Clergy Personality Comparison

| | Male scoring | | | |
| | | Comparison to male norm | | |
| Domains | Norm to women | Methodist ministers | Episcopal ministers | Evangelical ministers |
| --- | --- | --- | --- | --- |
| Neuroticism | Lower | Lower | Higher | Same |
| Psychoticism | Higher | Lower | Lower | Lower |
| Extraversion | Lower | Higher | Higher | Significantly higher |

In comparison, Francis and Thomas (1997) conducted research to determine if the more charismatic denominational movements, often marked by their evangelical bent, are pathological or psychotic. The finding was that more charismatic characteristics may be simply assessed as a healthy form of extraversion. There was no significant finding of psychopathology, based upon these comparative findings, among more charismatic leaders.

Other research compares evangelical ministers utilizing Jungian-type scales of extraversion-introversion, sensing or intuition, thinking or feeling, and judging or perceiving (Francis & Robbins, 2002). Francis and Robbins concluded a distinct preference for sensing, feeling, and judging characteristics. The research focuses in on a descriptive phrase that summarizes their findings which states "individuals who prize order, structure, and discipline in their outer lives" (p. 219).

Francis and Robbins (2002) explained that the ministerial characteristic of tenacity which may propel the individual on their career course may also have difficulty changing and responding to change. The individual is so focused on outer productivity and goal directed behavior that crisis and individual circumstances may not necessarily be as easily responded to.

What is clear through the research is that male ministers from across denominational lines are often more sensitive to the people around them. They may be described as empathic and sympathetic. While they may be tender hearted person, this should not be mistaken for their lack of ability to produce and be dedicated to a cause. One of the areas this tenacity comes through is in the rigorous training often required of clergy.

### Training/Credentialing of Clergy

The following is a brief overview of literature and research that is put forth on the training and credentialing of ministers. What does it mean to be ordained? The process and requirements of ordination vary dramatically from denomination to denomination. All denominations require some form of profession of faith (Finke & Dougherty, 2002).

Perl and Chang (2000) explained that typically a "calling from God" is the qualifying element needed for an individual to begin the process of becoming an ordained clergy. Furthermore, while a calling on one's life is relatively subjective, each denomination puts forth its own process by which the denomination endorses the individual. These processes include various elements including, but not limited to, approval by hierarchy of the church/denomination, educational requirements, and demonstration of duties.

Seminary is the term for a professional graduate school that provides ministry based training. Christian educators, missionaries, theologians, and other various religious organizational personnel train in the seminary forum. The Masters of Divinity (M.Div.) degree is the primary degree related to theological education for ministers of many Protestant denominations (Perl & Chang, 2000).

Perl and Chang (2000) explained that individuals who have greater levels of education are more strongly associated with earning potential in more conservative denominations. This dynamic is not a predictor of earning potential in more liberal denominations. Perl and Chang claimed this may be due to the fact that often time more liberal denominations have higher educational standards than more conservative denominations.

A call system is the process that is followed within a denomination for a church to receive a pastor. Some churches have ministers who are appointed by a superior (i.e., Bishop or District Superintendent). Other congregations have what is referred to as a congregational call. The congregational calls are when a local congregation has the choice to hire or not to hire a minister. This typically occurs after resume review, interview, and trial sermon. Education is a predictor of income in denominations where the local congregation has the ability to hire their choice of ministers (Perl & Chang, 2000).

Seminary education provides more than economic opportunities for clergy. While it may be a requirement in the ordination process, it is also credited for cultivating social networks distinct from that of the local congregation (Finke & Dougherty, 2002). The professionals often develop networks, similar to that of professionals in other fields, that is very different than those they serve. Finke and Dougherty explained the social networks, by calling them social capital, as an essential part of building a support network in the organizational culture where friendship can be built, experiences can be shared, and boundaries can be lowered to develop camaraderie.

Finke and Dougherty (2002) explained the process of ordination as entering an elite group of persons. There are individuals who guard the gate and let in those who will "play by the rules." If you get the right education and follow the right process, then we will let you in the club. This dynamic is paralleled to many other professions.

Finke and Dougherty (2002) argued further the educational standards do not simply create an elite group of persons who interact with laity; however, the educational standards create an additional social network. The educational standards provide an additional level of organizational culture that influences the individual. It is the network of peers. They have gone through similar training, met comparable standards, and been approved of by superiors.

The education plays a key role in the training and credentialing process. It may affect a minister's ability to gain churches and appointments. However, the real question is how clergy are measured for their ability to be effective.

## Clergy Effectiveness

Every vocation has stressors and determinants for which a person is deemed effective or not effective. The vocation of ministry is no different. Stressors to the vocation of ministry are unique and affect the individual. These factors play a great role in the individual's personality, vocational success and longevity.

One such factor is the relocation stress. Individuals may talk about stability; however geographical relocation occurs commonly for the individual in ministry (Frame & Shehan, 1994). The ability to be effective under stress is coupled with the stress of the family dynamic. In one movement, the entire family is removed from their social support structure and placed into limbo.

Lee (1999) explained that ministry demands are not taken out on the view of ministry. Instead, the demands are taken out in the personal global view. The stressors are not attributed to simply the vocation. Stressors are attributed to the behavior of people as a whole.

The impact of these demands is multiplied when one considers the effectiveness of a job that places the individual on call 24 hours a day. Darling, Hill, and McWey (2004) explained that to remain effective that clergy must have support to deal with their own life and stressors since they are always dealing with everyone else's stress and life. Darling et al. suggested creating social support networks that support the needs and growth of the minister.

The role and effectiveness of clergy are also impacted by the size of congregation and where the congregation is located (Nelsen & Everett, 1976). The impact of the size was the smaller the church, the more likely the individual was to leave the vocation of ministry. This may be associated with feelings of appreciation or financial.

Individuals leave the ministry for various reasons. Nelsen and Everett (1976) claimed that low remuneration was directly correlated to leaving the ministry, while lack of appreciation simply caused the minister to change congregations. The minister's work contributes to their sense of identity (Kennedy et al., 1977) and thereby one may conclude that if there is a lack of appreciation of the minister's work then this may be transferred to the sense of self. Ministerial work is a very personal work.

Celeste, Walsh, and Raote (1995) explained that the perception of the environment that ministers work in influences the minister. If the work environment is seen as toxic then the minister would want to leave. If the work environment is perceived as safe then the minister would attempt to stay.

Previously, the concept of testing and assessment of ministers was discussed. Malony and Majovski (1986) conducted a test to determine if the psychological assessments were truly an indicator of clergy effectiveness. They concluded the assessments were not. While the research did not support discarding testing and assessment of ministerial candidates, it did support for understanding the limitations of that testing and assessment.

### *Conclusions on Clergy Development*

The clergy profession places requirements on the personality like any other profession. This is a helping profession which requires the individual to be able to relate to people. This is marked through the personality trait of empathy. The feminine qualities often characterized in the clergy are not seen as a negative; in fact the qualities are seen as a necessity for their vocation.

Clergy are often a group of well educated individuals. The most common educational pathway is through a graduate or professional training. Primarily, this is accomplished through a Masters of Divin-

ity from a seminary. The education and training provide a social network for a group of social people.

There is an attempt to measure the effectiveness or potential effectiveness of clergy. Some research argues this can truly be accomplished. There are several elements that impact clergy effectiveness.
Primarily, the stressors of the job and the perception of the environment can impact effectiveness. Those stressors would only be compli-
cated if there is a perception of discrimination.

# Discrimination

*My father asked if I am Gay*
*I asked Does it matter?*
*He Said No not really*
*I said Yes*
*He said get out of my life.*
*I guess it mattered.*

*My boss asked if I am Gay*
*I asked Does it matter?*
*He said No not really*
*I told him Yes.*
*He said you're fired Faggot.*
*I guess it mattered.*

*My friend asked if I am Gay.*
*I said Does it matter?*
*He said No not really*
*I told him Yes.*
*He said don't call me your friend.*
*I guess it mattered.*

*My lover asked Do you love me.*
*I asked Does it Matter?*
*He said Yes.*
*I told him I love you.*
*He said Let me hold you in my arms.*
*For the first time in my life something matters.*

*My God asked me Do you love yourself?*
*I said Does it matter?*
*He said YES*
*I said how can I love myself? I am Gay.*
*He said that is the way I made you.*
*Nothing will ever matter again.*

(Anonymous high school student, as cited in Singer,
1993, p. 268)

Neat and tidy definitions of the coming out process give no con-sideration to a reader who has never faced the challenges of discrimi-nation. As pointed out in the previous discussion on the coming out process, pejorative cultural views of homosexuality and the coming out process (i.e., discrimination) encourage the repression of an indi-vidual's sexual orientation (Coleman, 1982).

Whitley and Kite (2005) explained there are three elements in understanding the process of discrimination: stereotypes, prejudice, and discrimination. The three elements all play in feeding each of the other elements in completing this process. In order to understand this section, a brief description is provided of each.

Stereotypes are simply snapshots of people without knowing them. They are based upon characteristics ascribed to groups they may belong to (Whitley & Kite, 2005). Schneider (2004) explained that while stereotypes have often been given a pejorative connotation, they are simply categorizations. They are neither good nor bad. They are simply the common attributes ascribed to a group of people. One would then need to add prejudice and discrimination to complete this negative process.

Prejudice is an attitude directed towards a specific group of people (Whitley & Kite, 2005). This attitude is often based upon the stereotypes or qualities one assumes that people in that group may have. Whitley and Kite explained that the attitude one takes towards a group is directly correlated to how one treats that group.

Discrimination can be defined as treating others differently based primarily on the fact they belong to a specific social group (Whitley & Kite, 2005). The prejudice and stereotypes are manifested in direct behavior towards a specified group. A female employee is not given a promotion because it is perceived that women are not as effective supervisors as men. In this example, the decision is based upon her gender and stereotypes of the gender which create a prejudice attitude that gives way to discriminative behavior.

Discrimination can occur for a plethora of reasons. Many companies and organizations have nondiscriminatory policies that may include, but are not limited to, issues of gender, age, race, disability, and so on. Gay and lesbian individuals are being added to nondiscriminatory policies by adding the term sexual orientation.

The attitude which leads to the discrimination against gays and lesbians is called homophobia. Homophobia is the negative stereotypes and attitudes towards gay and lesbians (McNaught, 1997). The term homophobia moved from a clinical term from its first inception to being a term used in society to describe those stereotypical and prejudicial attitudes.

The discrimination process is a psychological construct within itself. Therefore, this section will simply limit itself to a brief review of the literature on discrimination in organizations and discrimination as a choice. It begins with how discrimination exists, is perpetuated, and facilitated within an organizational culture. This will be followed by explaining how gays and lesbians have to make a unique choice of being subjected to this discrimination process.

## *Discrimination within Organizational Cultures*

Discrimination is not a phenomenon that occurs in individuals alone. Discrimination can be seen within organizational cultures as a whole, as well. There are several examples of groups that are the object of such discrimination within organizational psychology research. Those groups include, but are not limited to, gender, age and disability discrimination. An organizational culture that fosters the concept of stereotyping is what leads to an organizational culture that supports an environment where discrimination occurs.

One such example of discrimination within an organizational culture is the concept of the glass ceiling for female employees. Research shows that women are accepted in middle management, but there is a glass ceiling which prevents them from moving into upper-level management. In fact, women are often prevented in moving to upper-level management in a corporation simply because they are female (Chaffins & Forbes, 1995). Women are discriminated against because they are constantly put in a position where they choose between the traditional roles of being a woman and having a career (Herkelmann & Dennison, 1993).

Age is another issue that brings to the forefront the discrimination in organizational cultures. Nelson (2005) explains this discrimination comes from stereotypes. One may think an older person can not work as hard or is less productive. Hagestad and Uhlenberg (2005) went as far as to point out that discrimination with age goes as far as a way of segregation. Cultures segregate individuals who are older to do menial tasks while more important and demanding tasks are given to younger associates.

Research shows that stereotypes placed upon a group of individuals foster an environment where discrimination becomes part of the organizational culture (Boyle, 1997). Boyle examined the stereotypes placed upon those who were disabled. The social environment an organization allows to exist and adopts has a direct correlation to the development of its organizational culture. In this instance, the focus on constructs that was not congruent in truly accepting individuals who were disabled led to an environment where stereotypes prevailed and henceforth discriminatory behavior.

McNaught (1997) explained that the organizational culture's primary drive for overcoming homophobia in the corporate world and their drive to gain more diversity is the creation of more productive work environment. The inverse of what McNaught presented is the implication that a nondiverse or even a discriminatory work environment decreases productivity. The decrease of productivity would then signal an economic impact with an organization.

No matter what the public opinion of gays and lesbians are at large, it is currently legal to discriminate against gays and lesbians in the workplace (Whitley & Kite, 2005). Gay and lesbian employees face unique paradigms of workplace demands. Whitley and Kite provide the example of an executive placing a picture of his/her family on their desk. The moment the gay or lesbian employee does so then the outing process has occurred. This leads to a requirement in organizational culture which this author refers to as the unique choice of discrimination.

### *The Unique Choice of Discrimination*

Unlike many forms of discrimination, homosexuality requires a disclosure. No one has to tell you if they are of a different race or ethnicity. Many people do not have to disclose their disability or age. Whitley and Kite explained that unlike many facets of discriminatory practice, gays and lesbians have a choice to disclose their sexuality and therefore in essence have a choice whether to disclose this "concealable stigma" (2005, p. 371).

Most people do not have to disclose their gender or age. Rasmussen (2004) explained that a binary system exists in which gay and lesbian people in the workplace must either be out or in. The moment they come out exposes them to potential discrimination. They have to choose to take the possibility of this discrimination.

At the same time, it is a choice to reveal (come out) or not, there are many social manifestations that occur based upon that choice.

Whitley and Kite (2005) explained that simple questions become a conundrum of choices. For example, are you married?

The utilizing of appropriate pronouns is another consequence of that choice. The gay male who talks about his girlfriend to cover up the fact that he is gay is under constant self-scrutiny to insure that he refers to the "he" of his boyfriend/partner as "she." There is the invariable ramification that exists that every time the employee opens his/her mouth that he/she doesn't make a slip. Rasmussen further explained

> *The Gay, Lesbian, and Straight Education Network (GLSEN), the largest U.S. organization specifically advocating for the rights of lesbian, gay, bisexual, and transgender teachers and students...cautions students and teachers about potential problems that may be associated with coming out in a school setting. (2004, p. 145)*

These dynamics are not solely present in an educational setting. They prevail in organizational cultures across the country.

Some estimates place discrimination reports from all gay and lesbian employees in excess of 60% of the gay and lesbian working force (Croteau, 1996). The gay and lesbian employee must make a choice whether to come out and possibly become part of the majority of out gay employees that are discriminated against by their employers. This choice is a unique aspect found in the study of discrimination of gays and lesbians.

### Discrimination Summary

The discrimination process includes three basic elements: stereotyping, prejudice, and discrimination. These three elements are all indicators the process is in play. The moment stereotyping begins occurring then one can look for prejudicial thoughts and evaluations to follow. This is simply a step away from acting on those thoughts with behavior that completes the discrimination process.

Discrimination can manifest itself early on in an individual's life. Clarke, Kitzinger, and Potter (2004) discussed the impact of discrimination in the form of bullying on young lesbians and gay men. Children learn to stereotype and impose those stereotypes on children very early on in life.

Difficult coming out processes and the lack of support is cited as a potential reason for gay men to become sex workers (Uy, Parsons, Bimbi, Koken, & Halkitis, 2004). The harder it is to be who one is then it is more probable it will have a pejorative impact on the individual. No one's life is without difficulty; however, when discrimination impedes the acceptance of self, then ramifications may be severe and varied.

The discrimination process exists in organizations. The ramifications are a less productive work environment. Homophobia is one of the processes affecting our workplace out of the many discriminatory processes in play.

Gay and lesbian employees are under the unique situation that they must choose whether to disclose their sexual orientation. If the individual discloses (comes out), then they are subject to the discrimination process. If the individual does not (stays in the closet), then they are subject to the constant self-regulation of language and actions to avoid suspicion.

# Organizational Culture: The Church and Homosexuality

Organizational culture is a large part of this study. The overview of organizational culture allows the reader to understand the basic elements of research being conducted in the organizational and industrial psychology fields on this topic. This section explains what is organizational culture and how is it formulated.

A denomination refers to the different organizing bodies of peoples of faith. When there are differing organizational cultures that split the congregants of a church or groups of churches, then it often gives rise to the development of new denominations. There are in excess of 2,500 Christian denominations in the United States today

(Sherkat, 2002). Each denomination would provide a very unique organizational culture that would differ from others. This difference would be based upon beliefs, managerial structures, statements of faith, and other identifying characteristics unique to the denomination. This does not even begin to include the innumerable independent and interdenominational groups that exist. Churches may appear to be similar; however, if a closer look is taken then a unique organizational culture will begin emerging.

One element of organizational culture is the attitudes and beliefs of its members. An overview of organizational culture is provided. Examples are provided for the reader to understand how the dynamics of organizational culture works in a secular institution.

The next section will examine the attitudes and beliefs of organizational cultures on the topics of religiosity and homosexuality. Do ministers have a position on homosexuality and the church? This section presents studies that show how someone's religious attitudes and beliefs (religious organizational culture's influence) affect how they perceive gays and lesbians.

What happens when the entire organizational culture is gay? One area that presents a great deal of research is gay religious organizational culture. While the mainstream churches are not often discussed or examined to determine organizational culture without minimizing the sample criteria, gay churches are a niche within the larger churches which do provide some insight. This section provides a brief overview of such research.

Finally, the last section attempts to bring all the information together on organizational culture section. This section attempts to allow the reader to understand what implications this section has as it is all tied together. As one examines the organizational culture of a church, how does it affect the individual believer?

### An Introduction to Organizational Culture

Organizational culture, sometimes referred to as corporate culture, is the essence of what is acceptable and unacceptable behavior. It is how the morality is defined, the beliefs are developed, and the behavior played out. Schermerhorn et al. explained that organizational culture is "the system of shared actions, values, and beliefs that develops within an organization and guides the behavior of its members" (2000, p. G-8). Molenaar et al. (2002) defined organizational culture as the beliefs, values and behaviors that are shared by all members in a company. One can clearly see the pattern of the anthropological focus of these definitions. Waters defined organizational culture as "the source of motivated and coordinated activities within organizations, activities that serve as a foundation for practices and behaviors that endure...." (2004, p.36). What an individual can see, experience, and live in a given organization that is in common with all the other individuals who are in that same organization is how organizational culture is created, defined, and transmitted.

Culture can refer to beliefs, rules of behavior, language, rituals, art, technology, styles of dress, ways of producing and cooking food, religion and political and economic systems (Waters, 2004). Triandis and Suh (2002) explained that culture is the sum of the lived experiences, the interpretation of those experiences, and behaviors that become part of the society as a result of this. Triandis and Suh explained that culture impacts the individual development and personality of a given society. While some individuals impact the culture of a society, the majority of individuals are impacted by the culture. Companies are no different.

Organizational culture is a unique quality for each organization (Schermerhorn et al., 2000). Just like two personalities are not alike, two organizational cultures are not alike. The personality of individuals, the beliefs those individuals bring, and the make-up of those groups in any given organization are all varying factors that contribute to the uniqueness of each organization.

This uniqueness contributes to the idea that while one person may be trained with a company to do a specific job, that job will differ at the new company because of the uniqueness of each organizational culture. Schein (1986) explained that this is one reason that on-the-job training is so effective. It is not necessarily about training the person to do the specific work, as much as it is training them to learn to do the job in the specific organizational culture.

Plant and Ryan (1988) discussed how organizational culture can be developed at random by the make-up of the employees, or it can be developed strategically by the company. Organizations can actively implement programs and events that will foster and guide the development of a specific type of organizational culture or they can simply leave it to develop on its own. The question is not whether it will develop or not, it is a question of whether the organization strategically develops or grows at random.

Molenaar et al. (2002) illustrated this by examining three different construction companies. The premise was that safety was not an issue simply to be taught; however, it was an issue to be made part of the culture of an organization. Three companies were examined to determine if the concept of safety was part of the culture, meaning that the value and behaviors were shared from employees to middle management to executive management. It was determined that when safety was part of the culture and all persons shared this value, then the organization operated with more efficiency in safety than when the organization did not share this as a part of the organizational culture.

While the company that experienced safety as an organizational cultural value in the Molenaar et al. (2002) study utilized organizational culture for good, the reverse can exist as well. VanVianen and Fischer (2002) exemplified this quality as they discuss the concept of the glass ceiling in organizations for women. VanVianen and Fischer explained that women's inability to break through the upper level of management for organizations may have to do with the selection process, as most research has focused on; however, this should be examined from an organizational cultural perspective, as well. Values held by a company can limit the company, as much as they can assist the company.

Kinman and Kinman (2000) explained that organizational culture can come from internal influences in a company. Kinman and Kinman conducted a study examining the ability of an organization to learn. The claim was that if the employees of a company were able to be flexible and learn, then the company could increase its organizational learning capability. The hypothesis supports the fact that individuals influence the culture, in this instance organizational learning, of a company. What the employees do and believe has a direct effect on the organizational culture of an organization.

Sarra and Nakagashi (2002) explained that organizational culture can come from external influences as much as it can from internal influences. Sarra and Nakagashi explored the transition in Japanese corporate law to assimilate what is termed as the Anglo-American system of corporate governance. As companies are beginning to compete in the international markets, the jurisprudence system of each nation, as well as the individual culture of that nation, begins to impact the transacting of business. Japanese companies are adopting the general organizational paradigm in what the authors of this article described as taking the best of both worlds.

Dellinger (2002) explained that organizational culture can often times be confused with occupational culture; however, they are distinctly different. Oftentimes, professions have certain expectations of how the individual will dress, work, and behave. A medical doctor who walked in with dirty jeans and a flannel shirt who explains that she is here to talk to you about your surgery would not be keeping with the expectation of her occupational culture. The assumption is that a medical doctor would dress, act and behave a certain way. Organizational culture is not just what the professional expectations are; however, it is about the behavior, beliefs, attitudes, and so on of any given organization.

Organizational learning is one aspect of the organizational culture. The ability for an organization to successfully learn and apply the information from external and internal sources may affect the ability for the company to effectively compete in the economic markets of the corporate world (Lawson & Ventriss, 1992). Successful organizations learn to manage the organizational culture and learning.

Alas and Vadi (2003) conducted a study examining the organizational culture of six Estonian hospitals. They concluded that organizational culture was directly affected by an individual's age, position and education level. The individuals who make up the organization will define the organizational culture. Alas and Vadi claimed that it is not until after 5 years of employment that this study began to show that developed relationships affected the impact of the organizational culture on an individual. While organizational culture is touted as the secret element to making a successful organization, organizational culture is not always simply a top down decision.

Schein (1993) identified a few factors of basic organizational culture that came to the forefront: the interaction of hierarchical boundaries; operation of power and authority; role of perceptual defenses; linkages of forces across various other organizational boundaries; and the changing nature of the culture as the situation changes. This list does not purport to be all inclusive; however, the list provides a snapshot of those organizational cultures studied. These are a few of the factors of organizational culture that legitimize organizational culture in a research setting, according to Schein.

A great illustration of organizational culture being examined in a secular company is the study published by Raz (1999) on the assimilation of the two divergent cultures of the Disney Corporation and the culture of Tokyo's workforce. Disneyland relies on a great percentage of part-time employees to run its theme parks and in doing so has developed a very unique organizational culture. Part-time employees are recruited from abroad to gain the experience of one of the most exciting jobs in the world, as Disney proclaims. The Japanese culture values the relationship between the company and workforce. This creates an organizational culture, influenced by the societal culture of Japan, to have a job for life. Part-time work is not necessarily viewed as a positive thing. Tokyo businesspersons organized a franchise of the mega-theme park giant to open Tokyo Disneyland. The venture took a great deal of compromise as the companies hammered out agreements to develop a organizational culture blend that would satisfy the two very distinct, and what seemed to be opposing, cultures together.

In order to effect a compilation or merger of cultures or to affect change on an existing culture, it is important to analyze the culture (Allen & Silverzweig, 1977). What is the current culture and how does that conflict with where the desired culture needs to go? Some organizational cultures are steeped in tradition and morality that is the very essence of the organizational culture. Religious organizations are one culture where this occurs.

### Religiosity and Homosexuality

A unique aspect to the religious organization's culture is their statement of beliefs. Whereas Plant and Ryan (1988) discuss how organizational culture can be planned to develop the beliefs and norms, the purpose of the religious organization is to define those factors. Some may argue that religious organizations exist for the sole purpose of creating organizational culture.

When one thinks of a religious organization the thought of a peaceful and harmonious organization may come to mind. While this may be true, the politics that are hidden behind closed doors can be just as vicious as secular organizations (Burns & Cervero, 2004). The different theological perspectives alone, not to mention the managerial perspectives, have given rise to a multi-faceted division of churches into denominations.

Religiosity refers to the organizational culture of a church's influence on a person. In this section, studies are reviewed that examine how the two elements interact with one another. Does the organizational culture of the church (religiosity) influence an attitude on gay men and lesbians?

Olson and Cadge (2002) conducted a study with interviews of 62 mainline Protestant ministers. The purpose of the study was, when asked about major problems facing the church today, what the context of their responses would show. Even though gay and lesbian issues were not alluded to in the questions, two thirds of the respondents spoke of homosexuality in the church as a major problem. The respondents did not indicate their position; however, the clergy simply identified homosexuality as a problem.

Finlay and Walther (2003) conducted a study of undergraduate students which analyzed homophobia in relation to religious affiliation, personal contact with gays and lesbian persons, race/ethnicity, and gender. The strongest predictor on the attitude, beliefs, and how someone treats gay and lesbian persons is religion. Finlay and Walther explained that while the church as a whole may teach a message of compassion, the church reinforces homophobic attitudes.

Wilkinson and Roys (2005) built upon the Finlay and Walther (2003) study and examined if the context in which the homosexuality was presented impacted the perceptive reaction of the participants. One-hundred and eighty undergraduate students that self-report heterosexuality from a Midwestern public university completed a 13-item spirituality measurement, as well as, read several homosexual themed vignettes. Wilkinson and Roys found that as a participant's score increased on the spirituality scale the more negative the homosexual vignettes were perceived.

As one can clearly see, ministers and religious participants alike, have pejorative perceptions of gay men. This influence is traced directly to the organizational culture of the church. The issue of homosexuality and the church is an intersecting dynamic that gay and lesbians must deal with.

Yip (2003) conducted a study to find out what the perception of the gay Christian is. Yip found that while over 80% of those questioned believe the church has a pejorative view of homosexuality, over 80% of those questioned believed their own sexuality was accepted by their local experience of the church. This study provides an examination of the attitudes toward gays at both the higher church hierarchy and the local organizational church level; however, it does not address when the organizational culture is gay.

## Gay Religious Organizational Culture

The Metropolitan Community Churches (MCC) is an excellent place to review issues where gay and lesbian issues may be involved, while not touching the sample of this study. No participants were utilized from the MCC Church. The MCC is a denomination began for the gay and lesbian community.

The MCC denomination began in 1968 by Rev. Troy Perry (Perry & Swicegood, 1990). The church began to provide a safe place for gay and lesbian individuals to worship since there were no churches that would accept them. The MCC denomination has grown into a denomination with tens of thousands of members.

Many other denominations are beginning to deal with the issue of homosexuality; however, this section will focus on research of the MCC and other gay and lesbian Christians. Yip (2003) explained that homosexuality is a thorny issue that many churches would rather avoid. There are three primary qualities that exist for this organizational culture which are unique to gay and lesbian congregations in their organization and make-up: counterculture development, political constructs, and distinctive bonding.

The MCC and other gay and lesbian affirming congregations are counter to the traditional church culture. Sherkat (2002) explained that out of the 2,500+ denominations in the United States, only a handful accept and condone homosexuality. Many scholars will say the guidebook to the Christian faith, The Holy Bible, would be intolerant and would speak directly against this. This minority status of the church will create a unique organizational culture that must be addressed. This creates a need for the church to have a very strong biblical criticism available for utilization in training and development (Lukenbill, 1998).

Another aspect of the organizational culture that plays out is the development of political constructs. Lukenbill (1998) explained that as a minority status it creates a move to define and fight for equal rights. While other churches may discuss political injustices, the churches are not often the subject of the injustices. As previously discussed, the MCC is one of the few churches that accept homosexuals. The church not only preaches against oppression, they often claim to be the subject of such oppression. This can be seen as they cite Stonewall and fight for same-sex marriage rights. These civil issues bring a unique perspective to the justice focused churches.

Finally, Lukenbill (1998) discussed the distinct quality of friendship and bonding that occurs in the MCC. Sherkat (2002) explained the majority of individuals who attend and participate in religious organizations do so because of the family pressure and involvement issues. The MCC does not deal with this external family influence. There is no family pressure to attend the MCC church. The primary reason for the continued attendance is the bonding and relationship building that occurs between members. There is a distinctive bonding that occurs as a support network is developed among their members.

Furthermore, the organizations are held together by a strong values statement which speaks to the need of the individuals. Perry and Swicegood (1990) explained there are three primary values held by the MCC church: the messages of salvation, community, and social action. The focus on building a supportive community, which replaces the traditional family, keeps the members connected to the organization.

Perry and Swicegood (1990) also explained how the traditional church has been a catalyst for civil rights issues and the MCC church is no different. It is a minority-led group which is often focused on social justice issues surrounding the gay, lesbian, bisexual, and transgender community. Those social action events range from organizing the "March on Washington" to the acceptance of the gay and lesbian community in the National Council of Churches.

Perry and Swicegood (1990) explained the threefold mission of the MCC churches are not counter to the gospel teaching of salvation they preach. Their claim is that community building is central to the purpose of their church. Finally, they believe that their organization can not exist absent of social action.

This specific group of organizations has a strong focus on their social status and the political justice. The moral imperative that seems to define churches and their culture is not absent in defining the gay and lesbian congregations in America. Therefore, one can learn a great deal from this burgeoning organization.

## Conclusions on Organizational Culture: Homosexuality and the Church

When the author of this study began his research on the topic it was thought there would be limited research in this area. This area actually has an abundance of new research that is being conducted (Lukenbill, 1998; Sherkat, 2002; Yip, 2003); however, this research is primarily focused on subgroups of the church culture norm. For example, there was more research on the gay and lesbian congregations and their organizational culture development than for mainline denominations.

A unique part of this study is finding the difference between the generalized organizational world and the niche market development of the religious institution. It is more comparable to discuss nonprofit organizations in comparisons to religious organizations. Religious organizations believe there is a higher calling, and therefore when organizational culture is being defined leaders of religious organizations often assign a great part of the culture to theology. The organizational world may have some guiding moral standards; however, they have no superimposed standard of conduct.

Much of the research discusses the organizational culture from a success vantage. Organizational culture is described as that which assists a company to succeed or to fail (Bagraim, 2001). One of the common elements throughout all the research is the attribution of success associated with the proper implementation of an organizational culture. Tokyo Disneyland was discussed as a success as it navigated a merger of cultures. The research on the MCC Church discussed success from a much different perspective. The MCC's version of success focused on the element of bonding which occurs in the culture of the individual churches.

Schein (1993) pointed out that when the hierarchical boundaries are determined and crossed; an organizational culture is defined and exhibited. For the religious organization, hierarchical boundaries may exist as the role of the minister is developed; however, the focus leaves the hierarchical perspective of employment and moves into the world of members and volunteers. One of the primary differences between a general organizational culture and the religious organization culture is the setting of who determines the culture. Religious organizations are made up of volunteers and members. The employees of a religious organization are typically minimal. The members are the driving force of the culture that is developed.

Schein (1993) pointed out the factors of power and authority in the organizational culture environment. The religious organization typically has a setting or fixed belief of who the pastor (leader of the church) should be and how the pastor should act. The secondary issue that may come in the religious setting is the vying for political power. Once again it goes back to the idea of volunteer base of power versus the employee base of power.

If an organization wishes to manage the organizational culture, then executives will target groups of employees who share similar sub-cultures of the organizational culture to affect change (Lahiry, 1994). This clearly shows that while an organization can attempt to foster a certain organizational culture, it is equally advantageous to under-stand the subcultures that occur in any given organization. Subcul-tures can occur in both the organizational world and the religious world. Lahiry discussed the subcultures in the organizational culture of organizations, and Sherkat (2002) discussed the subculture of the gay male participants in comparison to the lesbian involvement in a congregation.

A unique aspect of organizational culture is the construct of occu-pational culture (Dellinger, 2002). The occupational culture of the minister would be what the organizational culture expects of the minister. How should a minister act, dress, or behave? Mulder gave seven examples of what may be expected of the ideal minister:

> *An open, affirming style; care for people under stress; congregational leadership; the ability to be a theologian in life and thought; a ministry based on a personal commitment of faith; skill in developing fellowship and worship; and denominational awareness and collegiality. (1980, p.228)*

Organizational culture is a vital part of any organization. The research shows that ignorance of the facts will only lead in a potential failure as the culture will grow whatever way it wishes. It behooves leaders and readers to understand and continue the research that has begun.

# 3

# *METHODOLOGY*

## Restatement of Purpose

This research desires to examine the lived experience of the coming out process in a religious organizational culture for gay, male, Protestant clergy. The research examines a specific event (the phenomenon of coming out) that occurs in a specific setting (religious organizational culture) for the leaders of that religious culture.

Chronicle, MacGregor, and Ormerod (2004) explained that many question whether the concept of insight has any contribution to the problem solving ability. How does asking for the experience of gay religious leaders give insight? Does this really contribute to theory or does it just describe specific events in people's life? This is a question the research must work through.

In developing the role of the evaluator for the research, it is essential to review the purpose of the research being presented. Patton (1997) explained that a combination of active-reactive-adaptive model, while criticized for utilizing more than one role, gives a well rounded perspective and provides sense to the study. Patton allowed the evaluator's own personal experience to enter into the realm of research. Therefore, the research design is designed with the purpose of the research in mind.

# Research Design

As previously discussed, this researcher conducted a qualitative dissertation utilizing a heuristic model as set forth by Moustakas (1990). The heuristic model is utilized in order to fill in a void where the research stops. There is research on the coming out process and the organizational cultural development of gay Christians and gay Churches; however, there is no exploration of what it is like for the leaders (the ministers) in the Church to have to come out. Therefore, heuristics fills the void and begins the exploration of this lived experience.

Furthermore, the research question is attempting to examine a specific phenomenon. This requires the researcher to employ a model of the phenomenological method. The heuristic model of research is a type of phenomenological research that is utilized when the research becomes one of the contributing participants (Patton, 2002). In order to be open and forthcoming, the researcher fits the sample himself. Therefore, it is the choice of this researcher to do a heuristic study.

In qualitative research that utilizes the extensive process of heuristics it is important to maintain a manageable number or participants, so the data do not become overwhelming. There is a great deal of processing that occurs with the interview transcripts. As themes and patterns are identified, it is essential to maintain the effectiveness of the researcher by not overloading the data. Upon discourse with colleagues and advisors, this researcher chose to utilize eight participants.

As a gay, male, Protestant religious leader, this researcher is part of the sample, as well. The researcher has personal experiences that influence how he views things. Therefore the research will attempt to integrate the experiences of the researcher by applying a heuristic model of phenomenological research. This is done so the research is not telling of the researcher's story; however, it is to tell the stories of the participants and to compare, contrast, and critically evaluate the scenarios to find the impact of the religious organizational culture on the phenomena of coming out for religious leaders. In keeping with the heuristic model, the researcher inserted himself as one of the subjects.

The evaluation would need to be an external evaluation. Patton (1997) explained that an external evaluation is when the individual evaluating is outside the program or organization being evaluated. Since this research is evaluating the impact on their life, this makes the researcher external to their life, thereby creating an external evaluation stand. This is an important factor to create a valid piece of psychological research. The primary source of information comes through external evaluation and not from the researcher himself.

In some form or fashion the results are individualized to the subject. The research is being completed in order to determine and document the process of development and its influential factors for this specified group. It was done by face to face interviews and involved contact with individuals and understanding their first hand experience of this development. Patton (2002) explained this is a responsive approach to evaluation. The research is a response to the phenomena that is being studied.

Every research methodology must have a defined structure of steps to complete. This replicable format allows one scientist to conduct studies that have similarities with others and to design new research studies. The steps to conduct a heuristic inquiry are initial engagement, immersion, incubation, illumination, explication, and creative synthesis (Moustakas, 1990).

Moustakas (1990) explained that in every person there is a question which is passionate and needs to be answered. The initial engagement is when the researcher begins a self-dialogue and searches oneself to find what one is truly passionate about. This is not something in which the individual is simply interested; however, it is something the researcher must become so passionate about that they can live with the topic as it permeates every boundary of their life. The initial engagement is when the researcher is searching for this passion.

Over the past several months, this researcher worked with the faculty of Capella University to assist in finding how to channel the passion into a question. This stage of research is brainstorming and writing down topics of interest to the researcher. Then it becomes a question of which of the topics written out is passionate. The researcher ruled out several topics and then met with faculty and supervisors to hone down a clear topic.

Immersion is when the researcher gets a sense of total involvement with the research theme or question (Douglass & Moustakas, 1985). The question has been found and now the researcher begins immersing oneself in the whole of the topic. Moustakas (1990) explained this is the stage where the researcher eats, sleeps, walks, and even dreams with the topic in mind. It is the actual permeation that is occurring as the researcher begins having a relationship with the question. Perhaps this is where Dr. Kostere (2004) explained that the process is like poetry.

Incubation is a period in which the researcher steps back from the topic (the immersion) and begins to contemplate its very existence and what it could mean (Moustakas, 1990). Moustakas parallels this process as to an individual who has lost one's keys. It is only when one stops looking, steps back, and begins things anew that it will finally come to the individual where those keys are placed. This stage is the stepping back phase.

Illumination is not the choice of the researcher, however it is the natural occurrence of the "eureka" moment. Illumination is when, through the natural process of letting the topic remain in the incubation of thought, it truly becomes visible to the researcher. All the other phases are choices made by the researcher. It is the choice to look for the passionate topic. It is the choice to immerse oneself. It is the choice to step back and begin incubation. The illumination is when the research reveals itself to the researcher.

Explication is when the researcher, after having the eureka moment, comes back to the material to pull the information from it that supports the illumination (Moustakas, 1990). Moustakas described this phase as an examination of that which was awakened in consciousness to find its several layers of information that it has to give to the researcher.

The final stage is creative synthesis. Creative synthesis is when the researcher must put it all back together. From the initial engagement to the explication, a process of learning has occurred. The layers of information that have formed in themes and patterns to the researcher are created to display, often in narrative form, the lived reality of the subjects.

Epoche is not included in the stages of a heuristic study, as presented by Moustakas (1990). However, this researcher is adding in the phenomenological stage of epoche. The epoche is process of removing the researcher bias.

# Target Population

The target population for this study was (a) gay, (b) male, (c) Protestant, and (d) ordained clergy. Some clergy may currently be serving and others may have left the church; however, the participants must have begun the coming out process while serving in some capacity of ministry of the church. There will be a diversity of denominations.

## Selection of Participants

The researcher contacted several potential participants known to the researcher as openly gay ministers utilizing a phone script (see Appendix A). These potential participants have attended conferences, programs, or other various public functions and identified themselves as openly gay. The researcher, being a member of this community, had first hand knowledge of these persons through conferences and programs where they have spoken or participated. Once the participant had been asked by the researcher to participate in the study, he was provided a page outlining the study and the selection criteria (see Appendix B). He can choose to participate or not.

The researcher used purposeful sampling to create a diverse sample. Denominational background was considered in choosing the eight participants. Individuals were chosen to create a diversity of denominational backgrounds, ethnic diversity and diversity of ages.

If there were not enough participants known to this researcher, then snowball sampling will be implemented. Snowball sampling is exploring an individual's social network in order to gain other individuals who may qualify for a study (Browne, 2005). Browne explained that snowball sampling may need to be implemented when a population is hidden or not easily accessible. The ministers known to the researcher were all contacted and informed of the need of participants for this study. If they were not interested, then they were asked for referrals to contact someone else to participate. This process was sure to produce more than enough participants for this study.

## Variables

As this research project is a qualitative dissertation, there were no quantifiable variables to discuss.

# Measures

As this research project is a qualitative dissertation, there were no quantifiable measures being utilized. However, the researcher did examine the text of the transcripted interviews in the incubation and immersion stages of the research process. As themes and patterns began to emerge, all the documents were examined and the researcher quantified the number of times each theme and pattern appeared.

# Procedures

The research was conducted with eight participants, including the researcher. Each participant was given a purpose of study (see Appendix B) and an informed consent form (see Appendix C). An extensive interview was conducted by the researcher in which a standardized open-ended interview (see Appendix D) was conducted and audio-taped by two recording devices. Two devices were used in case of mechanical or technical failure of one source of data, and then a set of back-up data would exist.

A standardized open-ended interview is when the questions are formatted prior to the interview and all interviews are given utilizing the same questions and the order of the questions is the same (Patton, 2002). This methodology is utilized when the respondents are being solicited for information, and you wish to ensure that a comprehensive and exacting standard is needed. The structured format provides a consistent approach; however, it also becomes structurally limiting. It becomes structurally limiting in the fact that the interviewer can not ask follow up questions. The interviewer is limited to the structured format which is given beforehand.

Patton (2002) explained the open-ended questions makes analysis easier as the researcher finds and compares information. Since the research is requiring and attempting to draw conclusions on development, this would provide a greater sense of generalizability. The research seeks to identify specific factors of influence and therefore can not leave these to be drawn from random questions but should be identified through a systematic and thoroughly developed interview. The open-ended questions provide the interviewees the liberty to answer from their own personalized perspective while guiding them through the exacting standards required for this research.

The interview questions were field tested prior to their exposure to the participants. A draft copy of the prospectus was given to six individuals to read. Each reader then provided feedback (see Appendix D) on the questions being asked, order of questions, and phrasing of questions to determine whether the questions elicited the depth of response and did not provide leading or limited scope of answerability. The readers were two persons from the mental health field, two persons who were active clergy and two persons who identified themselves as openly gay. No person in this group fulfilled the requirements to participate in the study as a participant. The feedback was integrated to create the final draft of questions which was utilized.

Since the participants of the research have been a marginalized group which has been and continue to be the object of discrimination, it was essential to create a safe and secure environment where the interview took place. Patton (2002) explained one of the benefits of this interview strategy is this very thing; questions can be viewed prior to the interview by the interviewees. This researcher attempted to create this safe and secure environment by providing the research questions in advance. The interviewees had the option to have the interview conducted in their home or office. Once the interview was set up, the audio recording devices will be removed from direct sight. All of these actions are taken to assist each participant in feeling safe and secure.

Patton (2002) explained that an interviewer can concentrate on the material being given rather than the next question being asked. It is imperative to listen and gain the insight being provided by the interviewees rather than working on concentrating on your next question.

Once the interviews were completed, one of the tapes was placed in a secure location as an emergency back up. The second tape was sent to a professional confidential transcriptionist that was contracted to transcribe all the interviews in a timely manner. The text of the transcripts and the audio tape were then sent by certified mail to the researcher for the analysis of the data.

A duplicate copy of the transcription was placed in a secure location and served as an emergency back up. The additional transcripts, which shall be referred to as the working transcripts, was secured under lock and key at all times when not in use. Furthermore, the audiotapes, once returned, were secured, as well.

A copy of the text of their own interview was sent to each participant. Each participant was asked to review the transcription of their interview and provide any additional feedback they may wish to offer. This offered each participant the opportunity to clarify any statement they felt came out wrong or wished to illuminate in depth any more. They did this by providing any additional reflections or comments in writing. These additional comments were typed up by the researcher and added as an addendum to their original interview transcript.

All electronic files were maintained on a jump drive, which was locked up when not in use. Electronic files were not loaded onto any computer hard drive to ensure the confidentiality of all the data.

Upon conclusion of the research, all hard copies of the transcripts, audio files, and electronic media were secured in a bank vault. After 7 years, all research data will be destroyed.

## Data Collection and Analysis

Phenomenological analysis seeks to create meaning and structure of a lived experience (Patton, 2002). Heuristic research attempts to examine a lived experience while understanding the researcher is one of the participants. For the purpose of the research study, it was necessary to analyze the interaction of coming out and the organizational culture of religious organizations for gay, male, Protestant clergy. The study seeks to create meaning out of the lived experience of coming out in an organizational culture that views this developmental process pejoratively.

The purpose in this analysis was to analyze the subjective experiences in the life of the gay male clergy. Therefore, the data must be correlated and grouped together to create a cohesive set of data whereby conclusions can be made by giving equal weight to each phrase (Patton, 2002). For the current study, this was accomplished by utilizing the standardized open-ended interview whereby the data was precategorized by the formatting of questions. Priest (2002) explained that it is imperative that all categories of data are viewed equally.

Heuristic analysis should be accomplished with persons who have lived the experienced and are being examined in a way which ensures a spontaneous response to capture the true essence of that experience so analysis can truly occur (Priest, 2002). The work can seem subjective; however, it is the analysis process utilized that creates a stronger validity and reliability.

In order to effectively implement the epoche stage in this research process, the researcher conducted the interview with the researcher first. This allowed the researcher's data to be included and yet not influenced by the other participants. The researcher was ask each question and then proceeded to answer. This was done out loud and recorded. It was transcribed and put into the data to be analyzed. Then for the remaining interviews the researcher simply asked the same standardized questions. This separated any influence the researcher had on the other interviews and results of this study.

The researcher sat down with the text of the interviews and read through each text once. This familiarized the researcher with the information of the text. Then the immersion process began. The researcher spread the transcripts out and examined them for common themes. Common themes were color coded and highlighted. Once themes were identified then the researcher searched for patterns of words within each theme. This attempted to identify any language that was specific to the identified theme.

After the researcher completed the illumination and explication phases of the data analysis, then the transcripts were turned over to another doctoral student with Capella University. The doctoral student read through the transcripts and conducted the illumination and explication of themes and patterns, also. This provided a third party interpretation from someone who was not necessarily involved within this phenomenon to be an objective researcher.

# Expected Findings

The researcher expected for this research to contribute to the body of knowledge and provide an initial view into the lived experience of this phenomena. The research is expected to provide a detailed description of the coming out process for gay, male, Protestant clergy.

The research is expected to see how gay, male, Protestant clergy identify the organizational culture they work in. Previous research (Lukenbill, 1998; Perry & Swicegood, 1990; Sherkat, 2002; Yip, 2003) has identified the church as a nonsupportive and hostile environment. It would only be logical to expect that leaders who are experiencing this environment would identify in a similar way.

How does the level of support of the church affect an individual's experience of the stages of the coming out process? Coleman (1982) explained the closer the relationship between the individual coming out the greater the influence, both positive and negative, the individual has. Therefore, it would be expected that individuals who have devoted their life to a calling in an organization and who were not received well, would experience a personally devastating outcome and one that works to set back self identity development, whether through repressive or suppressive behavior.

The research is expected to answer the question of how one reconciles their belief structure with their sense of identity. Coleman (1982) and Van Loon (2003) explained that the integration of their work, faith, and culture depends on the reception they receive. Therefore, if there is not a positive reception of their sexuality, then it might be expected that the sexuality would be rejected or altered, or their faith and belief structure would be rejected or altered, since it is expected that both can not exist simultaneously if they are in direct contradiction to one another. However, this study only addresses people who identify themselves as openly gay. Therefore, this study neither addresses nor purports to address the individuals who have chosen not to identify themselves as gay.

# 4

# *DATA COLLECTION AND ANALYSIS*

## Organization of the Results Section

The results section of this report is divided into four sections: introduction of participants, interviews, qualitative analysis of the text data, and conclusion. Each section includes excerpts of the interviews, as it is interwoven by the researcher into patterns and themes that emerge to create a larger exposure of the experience.

The first is an introduction to the participants without whom this study would not have been possible. A short introduction is provided by extrapolating pieces of the interview to allow the reader to gain a brief understanding of each of the participants. The introduction will include pieces of information to provide a snap shot of the individual and provide a sense of who the person is. The introduction will not include any key information because each participant's identity is kept anonymous.

The second section is the interviews. The interview section utilizes the actual questions of the interview as a template for its layout. The responsive text to each question then follows each question in part or in whole. Responses that were short or simply maintain one train of thought are included in whole. Responses that elaborate on several points will be abbreviated to simply provide a sample piece of the text. As well, some responses are rearranged and categorized differently to maintain anonymity of the participants.

The third section is the qualitative analysis of the text data. This section analyzes the interviews to provide the themes that appear within the text of the interviews. These themes include: need for identity and association, leadership, negative imagery of homosexuality, and active relationships to the organizational culture prior to ministry. Each theme is discussed in detail with extrapolated text of the interview illustrating each theme that is developed.

# Participant Introductions

### *Participant 1 Overview*

> I came to this church, which is my first church out of seminary, with my partner. Never publicly made a statement because I was told this is how we were supposed to do it. But we moved into our apartment together. People from the church moved us into the one bedroom apartment. They included him in the life

of the church but it was unspoken. When he was diagnosed with AIDS and was getting sicker and sicker, more and more people were told because I needed to take time off. The majority of them were supportive. There were at least four people who could not support me and left. By and large they were supportive. They supported me through his death. The laity was great. They gave me time when I needed it, words of encouragement, lots of prayer support. Encouraged me afterwards and have been very accepting of my present partner. They have welcomed us as a couple.

One of the things that it helps me to bring to my pastoral work is that I am very sensitive to people's need for acceptance and respect...inclusion. It has really helped me in my ministry to develop a real sense of the power of God's love and to focus on that, and to stress the importance of living that out that it embraces all people. My congregation, I think, has been enriched by the fact that I bring to my ministry as a gay person a real awareness of what it means to be on the outside looking in, not fully apart of things. It has helped many of them who have felt for whatever reason in their own lives that they are not part of a situation that here they have a place. I think it also has made me more attuned to what people are saying, behind what the words are. One of the things, I think, that many of us who are gay or lesbian learn early on is how to read people because we are so careful and protective, especially when we are young. And I think that is a real gift to bring to people in a ministry, to be able to really be there with them.

## Participant 2 Overview

Well, I grew up in a very conservative church so though it wasn't spelled out directly, any sexual activity was frowned upon. One of the things I questioned early was whether my involvement with people of my own sex was due to the fact of feeling such a prohibition of anyone of the opposite sex. The high school that I went to, when you enrolled at the high school, it was a church related high school, when you enrolled you had to sign a statement that you wouldn't go to movies, you wouldn't dance, no sexual involvement, no smoking, no drinking. All of those things. All the things I loved to do.

Well like I said, there was prohibition on sexual activity outside of marriage, so that was so frowned on that certainly my sexual activity, I saw to be frowned upon as well. I don't think I ever really talked to anybody about it.

Later on in a much more dramatic way, I came out to the whole denomination in 1978 by making a statement at the General Assembly of [my denomination]. I went in and went on record denying ordination.

## Participant 3 Overview

Before I came out...public school, was very closeted however, I spent summers going to Fire Island, but definitely not out to anyone in high school. Went to...I was king of the senior prom. I was Joe High School. In college, wasn't until my senior year in college that I started dating a gymnast, underclassman...I think he was a sophomore and I was a senior. A hot gymnast, thank you very much. So my roommates and everyone around me but I didn't let it worry me too much. Normal life...and I traveled. I went to work right after college. I went to work for a Christian ministry in the national parks. And I was living in southwest Texas working with [a denomination] mostly and preaching because I was called as a student minister without really knowing much...having a local church or college church background. Kind of thrown into it.

The first time I fell in love. Really in love. And the first time I moved in...and that was with [my partner]. I first met him at a place called Tye's on Christopher Street and he was 11 years my senior. He was an old man of 35. And I was just 24 years old and he was great. He was a graphic artist. He quickly became family. The first time I was really in love and coupled. Coupled with someone I really cared about. We were pretty much inseparable. We would sleep together in a very small bed, a single bed [at the local] seminary where I was housed when I worked for Christian ministry in the national parks out of New York...It was a great new experience for me to be able to introduce people to my lover, my partner, my friend...[partner's name].

The participant revealed after the interview that his partner had passed away.

## *Participant 4 Overview*

I would say that there was a lot, particularly in high school, college and seminary...there was a lot of internalized homophobia. Because my understanding of things was that I really understood from a very early age that I wanted to be a pastor and there was this disconnect between wanting to be a pastor and understanding I was different. And eventually as I began to understand about culture and everything that I was gay and while I was not in any relationships their were homosexual acts that I did but not any committed relationships and then I was always feeling horrible that I had sinned and going against what God wanted me to do. So it's a real struggle for me.

I think when I was in my relationship. All the other times that I had any kind of encounters with folks, it was basically for sex, for sexual gratification. There was not a deeper level of relationship, the appreciation that two men can be caring for each other in a way that I had experienced with my parents, who are heterosexual, in the way they cared for each other and were involved in each others lives beyond casual relationships.

I think my theology has always been centered around self-esteem and the fact that we are loved unconditionally by God. As I have moved beyond that internal homophobia to an appreciation of who I am and who's I am, I think that has made me a much more effective pastor. I am willing to take risk more. I am willing to be honest with who I am. I am more open to different attitudes and things that different people have. Having gone through this process of going off the roster and being put back on the roster again, I don't take myself so seriously anymore. I am able to laugh at things and at my foibles and things like that. I think it has changed my ministry dramatically for the better.

## *Participant 5 Overview*

I probably had a reasonably happy and fulfilled life and thought there was nothing really wrong with it. I grew up in a home with a sister, two parents and two grandparents, so we had one of those intergenerational homes. I started involvement in the church at the second grade level and stayed with it. I did church camping over the years. I went to a [denominational] related college, [denominational] seminary, got married right after seminary because I thought this was what I was supposed to do. I had visited the whole notion of am I gay or not when I was about 20 or 21; and basically when the doctor said if you haven't done, said or thought of these things before then probably you are not. I forgot the word probably. So, I tried to make this all fit the way it was supposed to and never really looked back and never entertained the idea until I took a sabbatical at age 50 when I had been 10 years at one church, 25 years in the denomination, two kids at home in their teens. Figured this out when I lived with myself for 3 months. All by myself. Nobody there. No playing around.

I think I was always somewhat confident within, but I grew up very much an introvert and had to make myself an extrovert in some of the things I did. I guess I felt, like sometimes we say that you find your voice that you haven't had as you experience crisis in life or some point of your journey takes you to this place or that. It's just been a much more fulfilling life as far as being a minister and being apart of the denomination. I think there has been more respect for me because I haven't...haven't backed down from them. I have never felt I needed to hide it and let people think that it really wasn't a part of who I am, because it was just a strong part of who I am.

## Participant 6 Overview

I grew up in a small town and started to realize that I was gay in my early teens, like 13-14. Sort of like had that hanging over me but at the same time was dating girls. I went to the prom with a girl and dated girls in college and moved to the west coast when I was 20 years old after 2 years of study on the East Coast. I had family on the west coast that invited me to come out. Then during that first year out there, I didn't really go out because I was gay but I guess being on my own and being exposed to a wider gay community than I was exposed to where I grew up, I came to realize that yes indeed I was gay. That was when I came out to myself.

I have always had a good relationship with the church. I was one of those kids who was always active in youth group and loved serving at the altar as a server and had thought about seminary actually since I was a very young person, probably around 10 or so. I have always felt comfortable in [my denomination]. I did, when I started seriously looking at whether or not I wanted to pursue the ordained ministry...I felt that I had to come to terms more comfortably with my sexuality...my sexual orientation. There are many people who go through the process who just sort of hide it...and just kind of go through...however they go through. But, I felt I needed to come to terms with myself as a gay person and how the church was going to treat me as a gay person before I could pursue ordination. Hence, that is why it took me more than a decade to wrangle with that and finally get to the point in my mid-30s that I just decided that it wasn't going to be an issue for me.

## *Participant 7 Overview*

Well, I would have been ordained 40 years this October so the culture has changed, you would have to say. The topic did not come up at all in the early years of my ministry. Then it came up quite rapidly after stonewall in 69.

I was married, had children. I am a grandfather. I...that is a big question telling me about your life before you came out...I had always been aware of homosexual feelings and I went through a lot of analysis. Not entirely to deal with those but certainly that was a major theme. I was quite comfortable as a straight man. I enjoyed the benefits that go with that position. One of our children was killed when he was 9 in a car accident and the marriage disintegrated at that point, having nothing overtly to do with my sexuality. But in the recovery phase of that, I was aware of attraction to certain men with whom I worked. Even though I nearly married again, ultimately I became involved many years after that with a man. That was the beginning of identifying myself as a gay man.

## *Participant 8 Overview*

I was in the police academy getting ready to go to seminary. This was when I was able to deal with the issue and began accepting it for myself. Interestingly enough, other people identified that I was gay prior to the point I accepted it.

I was actually engaged to get married. I tried to date women. I thought if I could date women then I could take care of this and it would all go away. I was raised in a religious home and it was like predestined for me to continue the family business; however, I was gay.

All of my spare time was spent in activities of the church. I missed my prom in high school because I was doing something for the church. Or perhaps it was to simply cover the fact I didn't want to go with a girl. I was a youth leader, lay leader, and then went on immediately to become a minister. I told my parents when I was 12 years old that I wanted to be a minister.

# The Interviews

The standardized interview consisted of 21 questions. The first 7 questions were demographic type questions to develop a self-reported chronology of the birth, coming out, and ordination. Furthermore, these questions served to gain an understanding of what the participant was doing at these different phases.

In reporting the data of the interviews, proper names, denominational names, specific church names, and specific geographical points of interest were changed to neutral references to protect the anonymity of each participant. Each of these changes are noted by the inserted word being placed in brackets. For example, if a participant referred to the Southern Baptist church and this was his denomination then the text would read [my denomination].

### Table 4. Participants' Birth and Age

| Year of birth | Current age |
|:---:|:---:|
| 1936 | 69 |

**Table 4. Participants' Birth and Age (Continued)**

| Year of birth | Current age |
|:---:|:---:|
| 1940 | 64 |
| 1941 | 64 |
| 1957 | 48 |
| 1958 | 47 |
| 1959 | 46 |
| 1961 | 44 |
| 1974 | 31 |

## Question 1: What is your name and date of birth?

This provided the introduction to the researcher of the individual. Also, this provided the baseline for chronological dating to compare age/year of ordination, age/year of coming out, and current age. The names are not provided in this section to maintain anonymity of the participants. Furthermore, the responses to this question are ordered chronologically, rather than by participant, in order to help maintain the anonymity. The date of birth and the ages of the participants can be seen in Table 4. The mean year of birth is 1953. The median year is 1957. The decade which holds the majority of the participants, creating the mode year of birth, is the 1950s.

The mean age is 52 years old. The median age is 47.5. Three participants are in their 60s. Four participants are in their 40s. One participant is in his 30s. There is a significant gap, 13 years, between the 31-year-old participant and the remaining participants. There is also a significant gap, 16 years, between the 48-year-old to the 64-year-old. The latter age gap points out the lack of participants in their 50s. This becomes significant because the mean age is not represented in this study. The more accurate portrayal of this group is the median age.

### Question 2: At what age were you ordained?

This question provides the researcher with comparative information on the age of the individual and their coming out age. How close in proximity were they to coming out?

*Participant 1:* Twenty-five.

*Participant 2:* Age 26, I guess…1962.

*Participant 3:* I was ordained at…good question. I was ordained at 34…34 or 35.

*Participant 4:* I can tell you the year it was 1989 so that means I must have been 28. I don't know. I'm terrible with math.

*Participant 5:* Oh, 25.

*Participant 6:* I have been ordained 9 years so…huh…that would have been…huh…38, I guess.

*Participant 7:* Well, 24, I turned 25 the next week or 2 weeks later.

*Participant 8:* I was ordained at the age of 19.

Five participants were ordained between the ages of 24 to 28. There were two who were ordained later, at 34 and 38. There was one who was ordained earlier at the age of 19. The mean age of ordination is 27. The median age of ordination is 25.5.

### Question 3: What denomination were you ordained in?

This question serves to provide the researcher with demographic diversity as different theological perspectives were desired. Furthermore, it provides a foundation to understand the vast theological opinions involved in this study which may or may not affect the responses each participant may give.

There were seven denominations represented in this study. The denominations are not being shown associated with each participant to assist in providing anonymity to the participants. The following denominations were represented: (a) American Baptist, (b) Christian Baptist, (c) Episcopal, (d) Evangelical Lutheran Church, (e) Presbyterian Church, U.S.A., (f) Reformed Church of America, and (g) United Church of Christ.

There was one person from each denomination listed, except for the United Church of Christ, which had two participants.

### Question 4: What denomination are you currently active in, if any? If you are not active, why not?

This question examines if there is a change of denominations from the time the individual was ordained to the present. The number of persons that switched denominations versus the number of persons who did not allows the researcher to see if a denominational transition was part of the response mechanisms. This may not be the only factor in someone switching; however, lends to an understanding of the participant data.

In keeping with the issue of anonymity, the participants will not be disclosed as to their current denomination. All eight persons were currently active. The responses indicated that seven of the participants are serving in the denomination in which they were ordained. One person moved from their denomination to an independent church.

### Question 5: If you are active in a denomination, then what is your role in the denomination you are currently active in?

This question serves to examine the current status of each of the participants. Is the person currently serving in a role of an ordained clergy? Did the person leave the church?

*Participant 1:* Pastor of local church....

*Participant 2:* I am a pastor of a local church....

*Participant 3:* I'm currently a local pastor.

*Participant 4:* I am a parish pastor.

*Participant 5:* I am an interim minister. Having done four of those after some years of pastoring and now I am retired as of today.

*Participant 6:* I am currently Priest in charge of a small parish.

*Participant 7:* I am a retired clergy person. I serve on the local ordination and standing committee.

*Participant 8:* I'm a local pastor.

Seven participants were currently serving as a minister of a local church. One participant was retired. One minister, who was active, was retiring and serving his last day of ministry on the day of the interview.

## Question 6: At what age did you come out?

Once again, this question serves to offer a demographic perspective of what age an individual was at when they identify they have come out. The question also gives the beginning point of the self report. In theory, things that happen before this age would have occurred prior to the awareness or disclosure of their sexual orientation. Things that came after would have been accounted as events which come later than this age.

*Participant 1:* That would be a process. Came out to family and friends in high school, struggled in college and haven't been completely out since high school.

*Participant 2:* Well, I consider coming out a life long process so when I look back, some of my coming out came at about age 14 or 15. Some of it was denial for a while, right straight through college. I think probably my firmest statement would have been after I was in seminary and had considered even getting married and so on. I just couldn't do that and from that point on the decision was made.

*Participant 3:* I was out to most people my senior year in college, then I moved away...Very out at 24.

*Participant 4:* Probably...35.

*Participant 5:* Fifty.

*Participant 6:* Uhhh, well there's two phases of that. I think, one phase is when you come out to yourself, which was probably when I was probably about...hmmm...19 or 20. Then I came out to family members about 21.

*Participant 7:* It all depends on how one defines coming out. I did not have...I was not sexually active as a gay male until I was 42. I had been married previously. So the coming out process was very gradual to friends, siblings, parent, parish.

*Participant 8:* I would have to say around age of 25.

The mean age given by participants as the age of coming out is 30 (see Table 5). One participant gave no age whatsoever concerning the age of coming out. Therefore, the one who did not identify an age was excluded in determining the mean. The median is 25 and may serve as a more accurate measure since the mean may be skewed higher with the exclusion of the individual who did not identify an age.

Three participants identified an age only without elaboration. Two participants gave an age that included either a range or more than one age. In these cases, the lesser of two or the mean of three served as the identifying age of coming out.

### Table 5. Participants' Age at Coming Out

| Participant | Coming out age |
|:---:|:---:|
| 1 | No age given |
| 2 | 14 |
| 3 | 24 |

### Table 5. Participants' Age at Coming Out (Continued)

| Participant | Coming out age |
| --- | --- |
| 4 | 35 |
| 5 | 50 |
| 6 | 20 |
| 7 | 42 |
| 8 | 25 |

Three participants identified it as a process over a period of time. However, two of the three provided a specific age and one did not. The latter identified it as in the high school years.

### Question 7: When you came out, were you in high school, college, seminary, or serving in a parish/church?

This question is another demographic question which attempts to identify what each participant was doing when he reports the coming out process occurred. These data serve to provide the researcher an understanding where the participant may have been at on their career development process.

*Participant 1:* College.

*Participant 2:* Well, it would be high school.

*Participant 3:* None of the above. I had graduated from college not yet in seminary. And not serving a local church just attending one.

*Participant 4:* Serving in a parish church.

*Participant 5:* Serving in a parish church.

*Participant 6:* Uhhh, when I came out I was between my under-graduate degree. I had finished 2 years of undergraduate and was taking a break. I wasn't ordained.

*Participant 7:* Serving in a parish church.

*Participant 8:* I was...getting ready to go to seminary. This was when I was able to deal with the issue and began accepting it for myself. Interestingly enough, other people identified that I was gay prior to the point I accepted it.

Three participants of this study identified themselves as coming out while serving in a parish church. These three persons were working in their career field at the time of dealing with this issue.

Three participants identified themselves as being between educational pursuits. One identified a break in undergraduate studies. Two identified the coming out process occurring immediately before starting seminary.

One participant identified this process as occurring in high school. One identified this process as occurring in college. The college student was separated from the ones between educational pursuit due to his identification with the college environment rather than a break in that environment.

## Question 8: Describe the organizational culture that existed in your denomination on the issue of homosexuality.

This question serves as the first open-ended exploratory attempt to determine the participants' reports of their denominational culture. The question elicits the perceived culture on a given topic, homosexuality, for their specific denomination.

*Participant 1:* Since I have been in it, the official policy has been opposed. In practice is don't ask, don't tell. That's kinda the reason I have been able to stay in. The organizational structure/system always has said that as long as you remain quiet it is okay.

*Participant 2:* Well, I grew up in a very conservative church so though it wasn't spelled out directly, any sexual activity was frowned upon. The high school that I went to, when you enrolled at the high school, it was a church related high school, when you enrolled you had to sign a statement that you wouldn't go to movies, you wouldn't dance, no sexual involvement, no smoking, no drinking. All of those things.

*Participant 3:* First mainline Protestant denomination to ordain an adult gay man in 1972 by the name of William R. Johnson.

*Participant 4:* My denomination is more liberal than many other churches and denominations. However, the idea was that gays and lesbians were welcomed into the community and certainly gays and lesbians could serve in the ordained ministry, but they must remain celibate. So I would say fairly welcoming but not as welcoming as like the United Churches of Christ.

*Participant 5:* I think it's always been kind of mixed. There were times as I was ministering and growing up and so on that, I think there was an openness because people understood that our denominational polity means churches can decide for themselves.

*Participant 6:* Well, that's interesting. Uhh, right now with my denomination, there is a lot going on. Basically, my denomination has already resolved that being gay or lesbian is not a bar to being ordained or participating fully in the life of the church. And that happened several decades ago. So, my church has been ordaining gay and lesbian people...that's causing a lot of riff. Mostly culture riff between how the United States is looking at scripture on human sexuality versus how primarily people in the third world, Africa mostly and Asian are looking at homosexuality and the bible and their culture. So as far as the United States, it is pretty much a nonissue point but for the worldwide denominational communion it is a very hot issue.

*Participant 7:* Well, I would have been ordained 40 years this October so the culture has changed, you would have to say. The topic did not come up at all in the early years of my ministry. Then it came up quite rapidly after stonewall in 69. Then I believe 70...I forget what year in the late 70s, my denomination ordained or an association of my denomination ordained the first openly gay minister of a mainline protestant denomination and that created or contributed to a great deal of ferment in the denomination including of course a study on human sexuality which came out in the late seventies, I guess, was very progressive for its time.

*Participant 8:* My denomination believed that homosexuality was a sin, that homosexuals should not be part of the church. One of the primary reasons that I was removed from my pastorate is that I would not stand in the pulpit and condemn a gay guy who came to my church. It became an option to either openly condemn this individual from the pulpit or I must resign.

The participants may be categorized into three groups based upon these responses: open and accepting, qualified acceptance, and absolute condemnation. Open and accepting is for those churches that will openly accept and affirm the members of the clergy who are gay. The qualified acceptance is those denominations that may accept; however, there are conditions upon which that acceptance is granted. The absolute condemnation is those denominations that simply and totally reject the idea of homosexual clergy.

There are three participants who identified an open and accepting policy. Participants 3, 6, and 7 identified their church as open and affirming. Participants 3 and 7 identified their denomination as the first to ordain a openly gay minister.

There are three participants who identified a qualified acceptance. Participant 4 explained that his denomination will accept a gay minister if he remains celibate. Participant 1 said they will accept a gay minister only if he is not open about being gay. Participant 5 claimed that gay ministers will be accepted if the local church will accept him.

There are two participants who identified an absolute condemnation. Participants 2 and 8 identified their churches as being completely not accepting. According to these two denominations, it is prohibited and simply labeled as a sin.

## Question 9: Describe how representatives of your denomination found out about your sexual orientation.

This question lends itself to whether the participant revealed this information themselves or someone else outed the participant. This may play a vital role in the way the individual views the coming out process. It is a factor to consider, therefore the information needs to be gathered.

*Participant 1:* Most of the people who know about it within our denomination, I have told. I have made known to some key persons to get it out there before I was ordained.

*Participant 2:* When I was in seminary, I was very open about my homosexuality. Earlier, when I was under the care of a [denominational committee] and I opened myself up to the chair of that committee....

*Participant 3:* By getting to know me. When I was first year in seminary, I went to work for the national offices of my denomination...I went to work with...the first gay male ordained, so denominationally that was one. And two, I was a member of a local church.

I would regularly attend [church] with my partner...I got very active in that church. So other denominational aspects. I was also already then had become active with my denomination locally on the association level.

*Participant 4:* The bishops sent the Dean and another person to talk to me because members of the congregation had suspected that I was gay. They didn't know necessarily that I was in a relationship but suspected that I was gay, and so they wanted me to talk to them about that. Shortly thereafter, I responded to the bishop and told him I was gay and I was in a committed relationship. So I was kind of forced out to a certain extent.

*Participant 5:* Two couples in the church that I served chatted together and figured this out. I already knew at that point but only knew within a month of that time. They put pieces together that really didn't go together, but they seemed to at that time. Part of that was my support for homosexual issues over the years. When I divorced, that made them believe that this was indeed the case. It was at that point but I didn't know it before.

*Participant 6:* Basically, I have just been out. Uhhh, I have been actively involved in the church for most of my adulthood starting when I was about 21 and living in a parish on the west coast and had just been out the whole time. I went through the entire process in my diocese to be sponsored as an out partnered gay person. They have known because I haven't hid it.

*Participant 7:* I haven't any idea. I think it was just a matter of observing that I was involved in activities and identifying with groups.

*Participant 8:* They found out by someone else telling them. I was living with someone whom I had a friendship which turned somewhat sexual. When he was dealing with his issues of coming out in the church he reported me to denominational officials. At the point I was outed, I did not consider myself gay. I hadn't come to terms with that yet.

Six of the participants identified themselves as being openly gay. They live in such a way or support programs that would lead to people either assuming they are gay. Indications are there has never been an overt act to hide such behavior.

Two participants were outed. Participant 4 indicated that his congregation had gone to the bishop. Participant 8 clearly stated that he was outed.

## Question 10: Tell me about life before you came out.

This provides the participants the opportunity to discuss any topic of their life. The question directs them to discuss the pre-coming out phases. However, the open-ended style of the question allows the participant to go anywhere they wish.

*Participant 1:* Conflicted. I struggled with coming out all through high school. That was a time in which I was very confused. In college, I went to a denominational college so it was a somewhat conservative religious school. There I was told that my sexuality was sinful and wrong by some of the people. I tried my hardest to fall in love with a woman. Did not work. Near the end of my junior year, in that summer between my junior and senior year, is when I really accepted this is who I am. I came out and have accepted it since then.

*Participant 2:* Well, in high school there was some tension in terms of getting involved and feeling real guilt about it. Praying and asking for forgiveness and I would never get involved again. And yet I kept getting involved again and again. Kind of living that double life also when I was in high school because I dated probably at least two thirds of the girls in my class. But often would take them home from a date and go out with a guy. Even did that on my prom night.

*Participant 3:* Before I came out, regular…high school…public school…was very closeted; however, I spent summers going to Fire Island, but definitely not out to anyone in high school. Went to…I was king of the senior prom. I was Joe High School. In college, wasn't until my senior year in college that I started dating a gymnast, underclassman…I think he was a sophomore and I was a senior. A hot gymnast, thank you very much. So my roommates and everyone around me but I didn't let it worry me too much. Normal life…and I traveled. I went to work right after college. I went to work for a Christian ministry in the national parks. And I was living in southwest Texas working with Southern Baptist mostly and preaching because I was called as a student minister without really knowing much...having a local church or college church background, kind of thrown into it.

*Participant 4:* I would say that there was a lot, particularly in high school, college and seminary...there was a lot of internalized homophobia. Because my understanding of things was that I really understood from a very early age that I wanted to be a pastor and there was this disconnect between wanting to be a pastor and understanding I was different. And eventually as I began to understand about culture and everything that I was gay and while I was not in any relationships their were homosexual acts that I did but not any committed relationships and then I was always feeling horrible that I had sinned and going against what God wanted me to do. So it's a real struggle for me.

Then, as I got closer to that age, 35 or whatever it was, there was almost a dual life that I was living the life of a pastor where folks didn't know I was gay as a matter fact people were surprised to find out I was gay. And then the life in a committed relationship, as well. That was tough. Because it was hard to constantly have to change the pronouns and all the other kind of stuff like many of us have had to do...to talk about her instead of really saying it's him and play those type of things.

*Participant 5:* I probably had a reasonably happy and fulfilled life and thought there was nothing really wrong with it. I grew up in a home with a sister, two parents and two grandparents, so we had one of those intergenerational homes. I started involvement in the church at the second grade level and stayed with it. I did church camping over the years. I went to a denominational college, denominational seminary, got married right after seminary because I thought this was what I was supposed to do. I had visited the whole notion of am I gay or not when I was about 20 or 21; and basically when the doctor said if you haven't done, said or thought of these things before then probably you are not. I forgot the word probably. So I tried to make this all fit the way it was supposed to and never really looked back and never entertained the idea until I took a sabbatical at age 50 when I had been 10 years at one church, 25 years in the denomination, two kids at home in their teens. Figured this out when I lived with myself for 3 months. All by myself. Nobody there. No playing around.

*Participant 6:* Well, huh, I am going to assume this is going to have to mean about my sexual life. I could tell you the whole story of my life but I don't think that is what you are aiming for. But I grew up in a small town and started to realize that I was gay in my early teens, like 13-14. Sorta like had that hanging over me but at the same time was dating girls. I went to the prom with a girl and dated girls in college. And humm, moved to the west coast when I was 20 years old after 2 years of study on the east coast. I had family on the west coast that invited me to come out. Then during that first year out there, I didn't really go out because I was gay but I guess being on my own and being exposed to a wider gay community than I was exposed to where I grew up, I came to realize that yes indeed I was gay. That was when I came out to myself.

*Participant 7:* I was married, had children. I am a grandfather. I…that is a big question telling me about your life before you came out…I had always been aware of homosexual feelings and I went through a lot of analysis. Not entirely to deal with those but certainly that was a major theme. I was quite comfortable as a straight man. I enjoyed the benefits that go with that position. One of our children was killed when he was 9 in a car accident and the marriage disintegrated at that point, having nothing overtly to do with my sexuality. But in the recovery phase of that, I was aware of attraction to certain men with whom I worked. Even though I nearly married again, ultimately I became involved many years after that with a man. That was the beginning of identifying myself as a gay man.

*Participant 8:* I was actually engaged to get married. I tried to date women. I thought if I could date women then I could take care of this and it would all go away. I was raised in a religious home and it was like predestined for me to continue the family business; however, I was gay.

Seven participants discussed some form of interaction or attempt at interaction as a heterosexual. Participants 5, 7, and 8 mentioned heterosexual marriage. Participant 1 claimed to attempt to fall in love with a woman. Participants 2 and 6 discussed their attempt at heterosexual dating.

Five participants included high school in their response. Participants 2, 3, and 6 made a specific mention of their prom. Most participants described high school in a pejorative manner. Participant 1 mentioned this as a struggle. Participant 2 described high school as full of tension. Participant 3 described this as closeted. Participant 4 expressed himself as experiencing internalized homophobia.

## Question 11: Describe the relationship between the church and yourself before you came out.

This question attempts to find any connection that is perceived between the religious culture and the individual during the pre-coming out stages. The question is open-ended to allow the participant to describe any relationship they wish.

*Participant 2:* Well, like I said, there was prohibition on sexual activity outside of marriage, so that was so frowned on that certainly my sexual activity, I saw to be frowned upon as well. I don't think I ever really talked to anybody about it. I remember that when I was in high school one day I skipped class with one of my classmates and he wanted me to go to one of these fine art theatres. He thought I had never been there before. I had been there before. We went in and instead of sitting next to each other we left a few seats between us. Somebody came up and sat next to me and I didn't move. My fellow student was very upset with me for not moving. He then came and said he was going to leave the theatre. I told him I had no intention of leaving and he called me a queer at that time. Whether he really was attempting to attack me or a quick dismissal, I don't know. I certainly had a number of sexual experiences in high school and in college.

*Participant 3:* The church and myself...the church that I knew...I was raised Roman Catholic and then had a lot of issues with the Roman Church, other than what their stance is for human sexuality issues but lots of theological problems etc. etc. etc. We had a really cool and very intelligent Protestant campus minister. Full-time also Professor. He was great. So I got involved there and then I got very involved when I was...I worked for Christian ministry at the National Parks, so I was very involved with church and fellowship and that kind of stuff and was not out with them. Then I learned to wheat farm.... learning to farm in a wheat farm in Kansas. They had a one room meetinghouse that they used as church on Sundays. They asked me to pastor while I was there so for those 3 months while I was there during the harvest, I preached there for them. Then I worked for...[a] theater ministry and I wasn't really out doing that but it was itinerant Ministry visiting different churches. But still very active. I was always very active in church related stuff. It was always good.

*Participant 4:* Very good. Able to rise to the ranks, very much respected, able to get calls easily. Though folks may have suspected that I was gay because I was getting older and was single and not dating anybody those issues never came up as a question. I was able to get calls without any problems whatsoever, I was able to be involved in leadership positions beyond the congregation, in what is the district...and even in the national church.

*Participant 5:* I've always been very fortunate to have good relationships with the people in the church. They have always appreciated the ministry that I brought, found me to be pastoral, kind of withered in terms of working with their youth. I enjoyed that over the years.

*Participant 6:* I have always had a good relationship with the church. I was one of those kids who was always active in youth group and loved serving at the altar as a server. And, huh...had thought about seminary actually since I was a very young person, probably around 10 or so. I have always felt comfortable in my denomination. I did, when I started seriously looking at whether or not I wanted to pursue the ordained ministry...I felt that I had to come to terms more comfortably with my sexuality...my sexual orientation. There are many people who go through the process who just sort of hide it...and just kinda go through...however they go through. But I felt I needed to come to terms with myself as a gay person and how the church was going to treat me as a gay person before I could pursue ordination. Hence, that is why it took me more than a decade to wrangle with that and finally get to the point in my mid-30s that I just decided that it wasn't going to be an issue for me.

*Participant 7:* Well, I served two churches before I came out and my sexuality was an issue in neither of them. One of them was a vibrant inner-city church that flourished under my leadership. I was there for 12 years. Then for 5 years, I was the associate at a very wealthy downtown church.

*Participant 8:* I was very active. All of my spare time was spent in activities of the church. I missed my prom in high school because I was doing something for the church. Or perhaps it was to simply cover the fact I didn't want to go with a girl. I was a youth leader, lay leader, and then went on immediately to become a minister. I told my parents when I was 12 years old that I wanted to be a minister.

Participants 1 and 2 avoided the question. Participant 1 chose not to answer. Participant 2 discussed a story which had nothing to do with the church; however, the story was about a friend from his religious school.

Participant 3 discussed a conflict with the church. This is one of the only conflicts mentioned in this section. The conflict was attributed to theological differences rather than issues of coming out.

Six participants described their interaction as very active and positive. Participants 3, 4, 5, 7, and 8 discussed serving in the role of ministry in this pre-coming out phase. Participant 6 discussed exploration of sexuality prior to going into ministry; however, he discussed this as a very positive experience. Participant 8 discussed the positive relationship with the church as a way to avoid dealing with sexuality.

### Question 12: What was it like when you first experienced the gay culture?

This question serves as an open-ended question to direct the participant to discuss the exploration stage. This question allows the participant to answer from any chronological point, both in respect to stages of coming out and chronological age.

> *Participant 1:* It was liberating, freeing…exciting in many ways for me to be apart of where I felt accepted and where I felt that who I was…was actually valued rather than something to be (unrecognized word).

> *Participant 2:* I am not sure there is such a thing as gay culture, maybe gay cultures. I mean I experienced the local theater where people were hanging out, maybe that was considered a particular type of culture in terms of older men trying to pick up younger people. Later on when I was of age to drink, there were the gay bars. There was kind of a culture there. Later on, there was a church culture. A gay culture with the Metropolitan Community Church. I would say a lot of different gay cultures.

*Participant 3:* I moved to New York when I was 24. I moved to New York City from Alaska. And I fell in love with a man...who was very engaged with the gay community and that kind of stuff. With him, I went to the gay bars and realized there was more than a sex culture. I would think that you to a gay bar to be picked up. I didn't realize there is real life. Not just sex maniacs. It was sort of surprising and it was a wonderful awakening on a lot of levels and met lots of good people who are friends [the guy I fell in love with].

*Participant 4:* Well, actually I experienced the gay culture most and got rid of the internal homophobia when I was actually off the roster [of my denomination]. The bishop required me to resign from the roster because I was not in compliance with that which says that gay and lesbian pastors must remain celibate. I became an interim pastor for a local MCC Church. They really taught me through bible studies and through other things...how to learn to love myself, and that being gay was a gift from God, and it wasn't something I needed to beat myself up about and that one could be gay and a faithful pastor at the same time. That was really the first time I had encountered the gay culture. I had gone to clubs and things like that but I had not really been around a lot of out gay people until those 2 years...that I was working at the MCC Church. I don't know necessarily if this is unique to [the locale I was in] but I found in the gay culture...a lot of frivolous behavior, or very surface type stuff in wanting to seek social justice. It wasn't till I came to New York that I really begin to appreciate the social justice side of the gay culture.

*Participant 5:* They [the church people] put me in touch with someone who had come out at a later age and we both kind of sat there and talked about the why me, why now kind of thing. He told me what I had to do to survive this. He told me I had to get a fuck buddy. Is that word allowed in this study? That was the most preposterous thing I have ever heard because I didn't approach people that way or relationships or anything else. That is no relationship if that is all it is. But I did begin to go to bars because those were the only places to go to meet people. The church I was in was fairly open about drinking. At that point, they knew me and knew I was going. I don't think they suspected anything too much. But, it was a real learning thing and I felt I had to be there to be with people who were like myself because for most of the week I was with primarily heterosexual people and I needed to figure out what this was all about.

Well, it was interesting to learn things that I never knew and didn't know I could possibly be so naïve. It also made pieces kind of come together that never fit in the puzzle of who I was. It was always happy. Life was good. My kids were good. My family was good. I had great churches and had a lot of friends. I worked for the denomination on a lot of things. But…at that point felt I needed to connect with people who were maybe more like me. It was a good thing because I also connected with some others in the clergy that were out. The first thing that they said was, "We knew it, why didn't you know this before this?" It was a good experience all around.

*Participant 6:* Scary. I didn't really experience the gay culture when I was growing up. I was exposed to some elements of it but that was the seedier elements, you know…rendezvousing with people and things. But as far as the gay culture, I was exposed to that when I moved to San Francisco and at first I found it frightening because it was very intense there. The culture was extremely intense and very much a part of the culture of San Francisco. And I was still like 19 or 20 and found the whole scene a little intimidating. Mostly through church met other people who introduced me to the gay culture and found out it wasn't really anything to be afraid of and actually I fit in very well and was comfortable there.

*Participant 7:* I don't even know what that question means because I would probably want to engage in a debate on the very concept of gay culture. But I have friends who are gay. I worked with patients that were gay. I had colleagues that were gay. I lived in New York City my entire professional life. So I don't know, at some point between seminary and the first few years of my ministry I became aware that there was much more gay life than I had been aware of growing up, but it was just part of the ambiance of New York

*Participant 8:* Very intimidating. My image of the gay culture was something very seedy, very effeminate, very much not part of the mainstream. Those type of images repelled me and I couldn't figure out why in world I could be gay. This was not me.

Six participants spoke of the gay culture with a pejorative reference. Participants 2, 3, 4, 5, 6, and 8 all spoke of the gay culture by providing some form of pejorative view. Participant 3 was the only one who discussed a transformation of that view.

Four of the participants mentioned gay bars or clubs in their response. Participants 2, 3, 4, and 5 included the gay bar or club scene in their response. Participant 3 specifically mentioned the transition of a pejorative view to a more positive view of the bar/club scene. Participants 4 and 5 both discussed it as the place to connect and meet people. Participants 2 spoke of it in a neutral way.

Three participants mentioned the church in their discussion of a first experience in the gay culture. Participants 2 and 4 mentioned the Metropolitan Community Churches. Participant 5 discussed how church members were instrumental in assisting him to connect with someone who could help him.

Two participants expressed the need of identifying with the culture. Participant 1 expressed how it was liberating to be accepted. Participant 5 claimed that he needed to be in the culture.

Two participants questioned the meaning of a gay culture. Participants 2 and 7 expressed their desire to debate or engage in a discussion on the topic of a gay culture. Each identified several realms at which a gay culture existed.

## Question 13: Describe the most memorable "first" that you experienced as a gay male.

This question serves to have the participant elaborate on the first experience. The open-ended question, guided by the concept of a memorable first, points the participants in to describe more of their exploratory stage of the coming out process. The participants may choose to answer in this direction or create their own thoughts.

> *Participant 1:* Probably would have been my first trip to Fire Island. It was that summer between my junior year in college and my senior year in college and I decided that I was going to go over to Fire Island. Getting ready to go over, getting on the ferry going over there, getting off there onto...at Cherry Grove of course, just surrounded in a culture that I felt this was great this is where I want to be.

> *Participant 2:* I guess the first would have been when I was about 13-14 years old. I was a boy scout. The troop met in the elementary school. The main meeting was in the gym. There were some times when we were just left on our own to work on projects. I used to use that as a time to go with whoever was interested in going with me into one of the dark rooms and we would just carry on. That was about age 12 or 13. But I made it to be an eagle scout.

> *Participant 3:* Memorable first...the first time I fell in love. Really in love. And the first time I moved in...and that was with [the person I fell in love with]. I first met him at a place called Tye's on Christopher Street and he was 11 years my senior. He was an old man of 35. And I was just 24 years old and he was great. He was a graphic artist. He quickly became family. The first time I was really in love and coupled. Coupled with someone I really cared about. We were pretty much inseparable. We would sleep

together in a very small bed, a single bed at General Theological Seminary, the Episcopal seminary where I was housed when I worked for Christian ministry in the national parks out of New York...out of their main office in New York City. It was a great new experience for me to be able to introduce people to my lover, my partner, my friend....

*Participant 4:* I think when I was in my relationship. All the other times that I had any kind of encounters with folks it was basically for sex, for sexual gratification. There was not a deeper level of relationship, the appreciation that two men can be caring for each other in a way that I had experienced with my parents, who are heterosexual, in the way they cared for each other and were involved in each other's lives beyond casual relationships. So I would say the relationship with my partner was a first, it was quite unique and gratifying to know that a relationship could be more than a sexual encounter.

*Participant 5:* Hmmm...the first...probably the first time I was with a man. That was on a walking tour that I was doing in one of historical parts of our country. Someone walked up to me and joined me for the rest of the tour. Naïve me after a couple of hours said, "Are you gay?" He said "yes" and I said "good." What else do you want to know? Did we make it into bed? Yes, we did.

*Participant 6:* I'm going to make that question not my most memorable one but probably one of the earliest ones I remember which would be when I was about 14 or so. Somehow I hooked up with this guy. I don't really remember how I ever did it. I met him near my home. He picked me up and he drove me off to a place. The whole time I was kind of scared because I didn't know if I was with this total whack job who was going to do something weird. It ended up that we had sex and I thought it was okay. I wasn't thrilled about it. I wasn't particularly attracted to the guy and, huh, it was okay but that is one of my most memorable memories of the gay culture.

*Participant 7:* I don't quite know where to go with that. One could describe a sexual experience or one could describe a coming out experience or one could describe a community experience and I really am not, don't feel capable of evaluating them in terms of ranking them. I suppose the first time I went to a [district meeting] and participated as an openly gay man with a boyfriend. I have a very good memory, so there is a wealth of memories that I could call on but I will go with that one. It was in St. Louis in 1993 which was late in my coming out but was one of the memorable ones.

*Participant 8:* By most memorable forces went into a gay bar. I'll never forget that. I pulled in the parking lot after I had driven around the parking lot several times, I finally got enough nerve to park the car and go into the bar. I went in and remembered it was so smoky that I could hardly breathe. People were everyone and it seemed as though everyone was looking at me. Most likely not, but it feels that way. I quickly left and got into my car but before I could make it to my car I began to violently vomit. I promised God if I just got out of there that I would never go back.

Six participants discussed some form of relationship with a person of the same sex. Participants 2, 5, and 6 spoke of sexual relationship. Participants 3 and 4 provided an account of an ongoing love relationship. Participant 7 described a trip with someone with whom he was in a love relationship/partnership.

Participants 1 and 8 spoke of an initial contact with a gay cultural scene. Participant 1 spoke positively of a trip to Fire Island, mentioning Cherry Grove, the gay section of the vacation get-a-way. Participant 8 spoke pejoratively of his first experience at a gay bar.

## Question 14: While experiencing this first, can you recall any imagery, thoughts, or feelings you experienced about your church?

This question attempts to see if any connection to the religious culture existed during the experimental stage. The open-ended question allows the participant to discuss any imagery, thought, or feelings the participant wishes.

*Participant 1:* I don't think church was on my mind. I was discovering many other things at that particular point and I don't know if church was entering into it. Except for the fact I was studying to go into ministry.

*Participant 2:* About the church…the church was far removed from my feelings at the time of being sexually involved whether they were in the dark rooms of the school or something that was very common, I remember this very well, this took place when I was in eighth grade, of sometimes getting in the back seat of somebody's car while it was parked in the garage and carrying on with them in the car. But a lot of that was simply checking one another out physically. But I certainly was fascinated by the whole experience. And those that I was with didn't seem to be turned off to it either. I sometimes wondered, as I grew older, what their lives were like afterwards. I mean whether they ended up getting married, etc.? Or were there any of them that ended up living the gay lifestyle, as well? It's pretty obvious to them about me because going back to reunions and so on. I was very open about who I was.

*Participant 3:* [My partner] knew I was very involved…when I met him, I had been invited from the National Park in Alaska where I was working as a student minister with a Christian ministry in national parks…and I was invited to New York City to work in their home office recruiting colleges and seminaries for the Christian ministries for the Park ministries. [My partner] knew I was not just professionally involved but also very involved with [a local] Church and he was really supportive. He came to church with me.

*Participant 4:* About my church...I think at the time sadness because I knew how wonderful the relationship was and how sad it was that this could not be shared openly with other people and how sad it was that people could not appreciate the kind of relationship that God creates or desires for us to have, a life long relationship, just because it happens to be with gay people, me in this particular circumstance, that this could not be rejoiced and celebrated as much as when heterosexual people get together. So I think sadness.

*Participant 5:* A lot of overlays to that question, because I was in town to do a wedding. And while this was happening behind closed doors there were people arriving from the church for the wedding. That probably, how should I say, adds a dimension to it that wouldn't have been there in other situations. I guess as I interpret the question that you ask, the more important part for me would be to say, one of the executive ministers said to me, as I thought would happen because I knew they would be supportive, "Now your ministry and your life will be more authentic and you will be even a more whole person." As I was experiencing what it was like to have gay sex, it was something I had missed and never ever had anything like that before. So I was thinking that's also a part of my own wholeness. I was living a lie and didn't know it. So in that respect, the church was involved in all of this during that whole process because I remembered what this executive leader had said. Had some fears in how this would all play out in the ministry of church. And somehow at that point had the sense that it would be okay.

*Participant 6:* About my church...humm...no nothing comes to mind in particular. Whether a feeling of guilt or shame or something...no, I wouldn't say that there was. I kind of felt it was normal for me at that age to be exploring with sexuality and experiencing sexuality. I mean by today's standards 14 is probably old. Kids are doing it a lot younger. I just saw it as an exploratory thing. You know, sort of like dealing with my hormones and stuff like that. I didn't have a particular sense that it was an extremely a bad thing to do or a condemned thing to do. It is not something I was going to go to coffee hour at church and talk about but I wouldn't have done that if I had sex with a woman either or any type of sex. So…so no particular strong feelings or emotions about the church.

*Participant 7:* [My national denominational meeting] is a strange event. It happens every 2 years. Even though the delegates are supposed to be representatives, the sorts of people who generally get elected by the conferences are those who are in most agreement with previous resolutions passed by the [elected delegates for the national denomination] and are on the trajectory to pass even more advanced progressive liberal positions so it has something of the atmosphere of a tent revival and a political convention. It does not necessarily bear any relationship to the reality of local churches. But in the context, I thought of my church as progressive, welcoming, exciting. For the purpose of your study, I am probably skewing your sample because I had very positive images of the church when taking the church at that level

*Participant 8:* I felt guilty and ashamed. The whole ride home I questioned by I should be in the pulpit. I kept trying to cut deals and negotiate with God to get this demon out of me. There is a feeling of complete isolation and abandonment as you have to carry this experience all alone. You can't tell anyone and you are in constant fear that someone might learn your dark, dark secret.

Three participants reported that the church was no where on their mind. Participants 1, 2, and 6 claimed to have no thoughts, emotions or reflection on the church during this experience. Participant 2 explicitly explained that his experience was sexual and therefore had no thoughts of the church, at all.

Three participants made reference to a church experience. Participant 3 described his relationship with the church and how that involved his partner. Participant 5 explained that while his experience was sexual in nature that he was doing a wedding and the church guest were in the next room. Participant 7 described a denominational meeting with his partner.

Two participants described pejorative emotions. Participant 4 described a feeling of sadness. Participant 8 described feelings of guilt and shame.

### Question 15: Tell me about your coming out experience.

This question moves the participant into the coming out stage. The open-ended question ask the participant to reflect upon this experience and describe it, however they wish.

> *Participant 1:* Coming out has really been a process. I came out to different people at different times, family of course first. I am very close to my mother so she knew very early on and that was great. She was really accepting. To my brothers, next. Left Dad for last. I was a little more concerned about him but he's been great too. Coming out to people friends and little by little people were told. I guess it kind of seems so long ago that I really have trouble remembering the whole process. The church was the last place I came out.

> *Participant 2:* Well, there again, I don't know how to describe the coming out experience because to me coming out is a continual sort of thing. There was coming out to myself at that early age. There was coming out to some friends. Later on in a much more dramatic way, I came out to the whole denomination in 1978 by making a statement at the General Assembly of [my denomination]. I went in and went on record denying ordination. One of my friends, a fellow minister, immediately had a

motion passed that instituted a grandfather clause that it would not affect the ordination of those who had already been ordained. I felt terrible about that. I was ready to demit the ministry at that point. The only reason that I did not...that several of those for whom the door was now closed came to me and said, "It is important that you stay within the church and keep fighting for us within the church rather than leave." I had a number of friends that left [my denomination] at that time. Many of them ended up serving Metropolitan Community Churches where they said they "We're not going to fight that battle anymore. We are going to go where we are accepted."

*Participant 3:* My coming out...it is always...coming out...I don't think you can talk about one experience. Coming out is a lifelong process. I don't think you come out once and you're done with it. Unless you never meet any new people, ever in your entire life again. Never change addresses. Never change occupations. Nothing. I don't think there's one coming out experience.

When I was first accepting of who I was, realizing who I was, and willing to share who I was with others...coming out was a reluctant process of allowing people to see that side of me...But I was also surrounded with remarkably loving people, colleagues from the Christian ministry and the national parks...They were totally supportive. Just wonderful.

My brothers and sisters, very supportive. My parents blind to the fact that even though [my boyfriend] and I had moved in together, [my boyfriend] was with us every Thanksgiving and Christmas, very much part of the family, they were very blind to the fact that [my boyfriend] is my lover, until I told them straight out. So...it was a real positive experience for me. It has been and continues to be. At the same time it gives one cause for pause out of deference to the others' ignorance or prejudice. But I'm cautiously optimistic always and non-apologetic at this point.

*Participant 4:* It was painful because in the coming out I had to resign from being a pastor which is what I wanted to do for my entire life. Ended up moving back to [a city in Florida], to a community that was more supportive always sensing that I was somehow going to get back in ministry, the [his denomination] ministry. I always knew that somehow everything was going to be okay. But it was very painful. It was helpful to be able to go back to a community where I did know people. That helped me and my partner to get an apartment. I was able to get a job. Actually, the MCC Pastor at the time, who ended up leaving, who I replaced as interim, suggested that I go to work at a department store. I was able to get that position. Shortly thereafter, one of the other [his denomination] pastors needed a parish administrator. He said he felt it was a crime the way the church had treated me because of having to resign cause he knew I was a good pastor. So that sense of warmth, of people in my denomination who knew me as a person, accepted me, it was a very powerful experience. Even to the point of, in this congregation where I was a parish administrator they eventually wanted me to work with the youth group and teach confirmation. The pastor came to me and talked to me about that and I said, "Pastor have you informed the parents of what my situation is?" He said, "That is not an issue at all. They know you are gay and they know you are in a relationship. They have no qualms with you working with their kids and teaching." What a joy it was to know that yes in my denomination while the official policy maybe that I couldn't be in a committed relationship and be a pastor that I can function as a pastor and eventually work back into being able to preach and preside in [my denomination] again. So there was the pain and a sense of loss, but eventually a sense of joy that I could be accepted for who I am and be able to be a pastor.

*Participant 5:* I think I mentioned earlier the two couples sort of figured it out. One of them came to the office and said because you've been doing all these supportive things for defeating some of the anti-gay initiatives, you've encouraged us to sign petitions to get people to stick to [denominational] principles and the principles of autonomy of the local church and try to block some of these things. Now you are separating from your wife, preparing for divorce, and because you just taught this study class with another man and woman from the church on the bible and homosexuality. We think you're gay. And we think you are having an affair with so and so. Which was totally...totally not true. But, it was kind of a shock. I knew it was coming but I didn't know they had put all these pieces together and thought it meant what it did because I had only figured this out only weeks before they sat there. So that was a difficult time. I am a person who has a hard time not being honest with people and I could not tell them a lie. So I asked them first what they meant, what they saw, why they just jumped to those conclusions because it was all circumstantial. Only to give myself time to think about what I was really going to say. Eventually said yes I am but told them that I had just figured this out. Asked them to be discreet and give me time to figure it out. What it meant and where I was going with it. One of them said, "So then you might change your mind?" I just didn't answer that question. I guess they thought maybe I would put it all aside and repent of my sins and try to get my wife back and all that kind of thing.

But what happened was a very beautiful process in the end, a very meaningful one. We got together with two people from the church and one of these executives, an outside consultant, who put together a process where I had to share my story with everyone in the church. We did meetings back to back, several nights in a row, two or three meetings in a night, people could come in for an hour or so and have a cup of coffee, hopefully not wretch their coffee while their listening to this story. It was a good way to try and tell everyone the same thing. I prepared what I was going to say so that basically everyone heard the same thing. It was very meaningful for the most part to get a sense of where people were on it. Some people chose to share right then and there and others shared in the next day or so. And did manage for a whole week to do this. Then on the weekend we had two question and answer times when people could come to the church and just engage in dialogue. There were a lot of misconceptions. There were a lot of assumptions because I talked about having figured this out…because I had figured this out while I was on sabbatical that there must have been someone there and I must have been doing something with someone to figure this out. It couldn't possibly be something I could figure out intellectually or in my head. That indeed was the way it was. There was no one there.

What happened between the first and second evening of questions was that on the second evening it became a painful thing to lift one foot in front of the other and walk up the stairs into the church to meet with these people because I thought I really don't want to do this again. It's not that it was so awful but little did I know that one was going to be much worse than the first one, which was fairly easy. The part about the first one, the question and answer time, that was not easy, was that people had done some of their homework. They had gotten an 800 number for me where the Billy Graham Associates would help me get through this, if I would repent of my sins and so one that I could go on with life. There were a few other things like this that they had decided. The presence of one of the executives from our denomination was helpful because it helped people to sort of focus in on how Baptist handle these things. They begin to know that it was really their…their and my thing to deal with and no anybody else's.

The second night, after I finally got in there, there were some very interesting things that happened which were sort of humorous. At one point, one man sat in the back of the room and kind of wagged his finger at me and pointed to the fact that I was the problem and I needed to get out and so on and so forth. It was a very angry kind of thing. I knew this was coming from a man who had disowned his own gay son who was now in a 14-year relationship and had not really spoken to him in 14 years.

But, the kind of ironic surprise of this came a few days later. I shared with my wife, with whom I was separated at the time, what was going on in these meetings. She called me a few days later so I wouldn't be the last to hear that she was dating this man. They eventually began to live together. The good news is that she got him and his son back together. She is a good person.

Those were very painful times, but I came through those thinking that when the deacons brought a recommendation to the church a few days later that it was going to be okay. They basically recommended that I be affirmed as a person and as their minister and kept as their pastor. The percentage of the vote was significantly high for that. We probably lost four people...which was not a...not a major...I shouldn't minimize that, but that was not what people feared. They feared that whatever way it goes we are going to lose a lot of people.

*Participant 6:* Well, I moved to San Francisco and, huh, you know...got involved with a church that had some gay members. Became really good friends with them. They become a really good support system for me. And, huh...huh...sorta came to terms with my sexuality. I could fully participate in the [my denomination] and that was okay. The...huh...sorta got involved with this older guy when I was there. And, huh...I don't remember it particularly being a sexual relationship. I just remember it being a very good friendship. And then through my job, I met someone who I fell in love with and became a partner with and moved in with. This older guy got very jealous about that because I wasn't spending as much time with him. And as a result, he notified my aunt, who I was living with there, and also my parents, that I was gay. So, that was kinda a hard way to come out but it worked out alright. The way my aunt dealt with it was she was a little angry that I wasn't honest with her because she had no problem with it. She just wished I had been honest but when you're 20 years old or 21, what type of things are going on in your head. And, huh...my parents were at first shocked but my sister had them go into counseling over it. The counselor felt they were dealing with it just fine. They are a very loving family...very loving parents. And so that ended up not being an issue either. So that is how I came out to myself and came out to my family.

*Participant 7:* I am not sure how you define coming out or how one marks that. I was coming out to myself when I was 42. There was coming out to the first friend. Coming out to the first family member. Coming out to my mother. Coming out to my best friend since second grade. It was gradual. It was not trumpets like here is an announcement. It was with no announcements. I came out to myself in 1982. It was 14 years later that I sent out a Christmas letter making reference to the man I had been involved with at that point for 3 years in such a way that it was unmistakable what was going on. That went out to the 120 people on my Christmas card list which included relatives, friends, former parishioners and so forth. But at that point almost all of them, certainly those who were in touch with me, already knew. In some cases it was word of mouth, and for others it was just telling them later. There was no general announcement.

*Participant 8:* Coming out was an experience that happens over time. Some I have come out to and others still don't know, or at least I haven't confirmed their suspicion. I am not for sure if I ever came out or was simply thrown out of the closet. Sometimes I feel it was the latter. I remember being attracted to guys since I was very young, perhaps 11 or 12 years old. I often would try to rationalize these emotions out by saying that it was the type of guy I wanted to be. I couldn't ever face the truth.

The ultimate experience occurred when I was in [academic training]. I had been kicked out of undergraduate and fired from my job. Well, actually fired from several jobs. I had the wonderful pleasure of connecting with a psychologist for the state who talked to me after class one day. As we sat and talked, I finally told her I thought I was gay. She probably thought I was crazy but that is not what was communicated. He hugged me and let me know it was okay. I sobbed and cried. This was my first time telling anyone. I was safe with her. I am thankful to this very day that I had her in my life. She allowed me to be me. Then it was on to family. The funny thing is that before I figured out what was going on, others were figuring it out around me.

Five participants responded by including an explanation that coming out happens over an extended period of time. Participants 1, 2, 3, 7, and 8 included an explanation of their inability to describe one specific incident; rather, they explained it is a process, continual, gradual, and never ending. These participants explained that coming out occurs in multiple settings (i.e., in the family, in the church, to church leaders, to friends) over time.

Participants 4, 5, and 6 provided detailed accounts of events that occurred in the coming out process for each of them in the organizational culture's setting. Each of these processes was detailed with several events occurring.

## Question 16: Describe how a denominational leader reacted when you came out.

While the previous question attempts to examine the overall coming out process, the next three questions examines the lived experience of that stage from individuals involved in the organizational culture of their respective churches. This question aims the participants to respond in accordance with those person(s) in authority over the participant.

*Participant 1:* One of the people would have been the person who oversees our area. He was very supportive. At the time, I was thinking of leaving the denomination. He actually worked with me to convince me to stay in, to work from within to try and bring about some changes in the denomination. Since then he has also been extremely supportive. He invites my partner and I to all the church events. He includes us as a couple, regularly in all denominational functions. It is great.

*Participant 2:* Well, I think strong support. And the reason that there was strong support was because in 1978 when I took this nationally people knew that I had already made a real contribution to the denomination and they were very supportive of me. I still remember that when I made my statement at General Assembly, the [denominational] executive, which would be like a bishop to us, was not in the room at the time and I ran into him as I was coming out of that auditorium. I said that I wished he would have been present, I just read a statement. He read the statement. His first reaction was, "Was the press there?" I said "Thanks a lot. You didn't ask me how I feel or anything like that. You were really concerned about public relations." He indicated why and then we went across the street and we talked at length. He said, "We are having a dinner tonight with all the Long Island people coming together. Do you want to make a statement to them?" I said certainly. We had about 10-12 people from Long Island that were at that general assembly meeting. The executive asked if I minded if he calls his counterparts in all the [denominational districts] for the greater metropolitan area since they all know you. So I made that statement to all of them. Then in every case they came up in embraced me.

One woman, who I had always thought of to be very conservative in her theology…she came from the south. She came up to me she used language that I am sure she never used before. She said, "I was wondering how long you were going to take this shit." Then gave me a big kiss.

*Participant 3:* I was working with Bill Johnson and he was the first gay boy ordained. I don't even remember ever having to come out to him. And I was working with other higher ups who were all remarkably affirming and supportive. It was never an issue.

*Participant 4:* My former bishop, who was retired at the time, the bishop who ordained me said that the church was losing one of its greatest pastors and he wanted me to leave my partner, move back to [the state I was from] and he would personally pay for me to go into one of these programs to detox me, or whatever you say, because it was absolutely horrible. He loved me as a person but he thought I was, not marching into hell, but pretty close. This was the guy who had ordained me. He would do everything in his power to help me. I said well bishop, you and I are going to have to disagree on this point.

*Participant 5:* They were extremely supportive. As I said earlier, I guess that is why I went back to that one question. I went back because I wanted to say that part about how after listening to it they...I had the feeling that they did accept and affirm me for who I was. It didn't matter to them what this was because the person they knew was much more than just this one new piece of information. The one did say that it was her sense that my life would be happy...happier and more fulfilled and that I would be a more whole person when this was all said and done. I didn't believe it. Didn't believe it for one minute. As I went through this there were times, as I said, when this kind of came into my mind and I felt, "Well they are really right," because I felt the pieces coming together.

*Participant 6:* Boy! [They] reacted fine. The [denomination] has always I think recognized the gifts and ministries of gays and lesbians in the church. They have struggled with trying to accept that, and to be more open with that and to be more affirming of that although that come along why. It was not a negative reaction. It was one of support. I will say that I'm going to use the clergy that I talk to when I first talked about becoming a [minister], he asked me to seriously consider the idea of to of going as an openly gay person because he felt the church was not ready to deal with that. He advised me to wait on it and think on it and perhaps not to go. I continued to meet with on a monthly basis and within a year he was convinced that I should pursue it and go. I thought that was fairly affirming.

*Participant 7:* That makes coming out sound like a discreet process or event. The only denominational leaders I have much contact is with the local area conference minister. It was kind of an awkward situation because about the time I came out I was a candidate for this guy's job. It was between him and me. He won not, I will be so bold to say, on the basis of qualifications but on some political considerations that have to do with other factors, not sexual. At some point during his very long tenure in that position, I don't know how he knew, but I started being appointed to committees as clearly the openly gay representative.

*Participant 8:* I lost my church, I was kicked out of college, one of the denominational people said he heard a rumor that I was faggot and they didn't want a faggot walking around with a degree from their school. I walked away. It was a devastating thing to a young guy. I didn't know what to do, so I packed my stuff and left.

Six participants reported very strong and positive experiences. While denominations, at large, may have a policy in their polity against homosexuality, the individuals reported strongly supportive responses from their direct supervisors.

Two participants, 4 and 8, reported a negative experience. Participant 4 reported being removed from ministry and being offered therapy. Participant 8 reported being removed from ministry and called pejorative names.

## Question 17: Describe how your peers (either fellow seminary students or clergy) reacted when you came out.

In keeping with the examination of the persons in the organizational culture of the church, this question gears the participants to discuss those of equal status, colleagues. The question is open enough for the individual to answer in various settings along the coming out stage.

*Participant 1:* In seminary it was a mixture. There were those who were supportive and we formed our own fellowship of gay, lesbian, bisexual and maybe some transgender too. But we formed our own support network/group. Overall at that particular time at the seminary it was pretty supportive aside from the administrators who were of the opinion we should, that number one we remain quiet and then number two it would be best if we left the campus instead of meeting at a table during meal times. But overall, I would have to say that during that time the seminary was really accepting as were my professors. Peers were great. It was a very good experience.

*Participant 2:* Well, let me deal with the latter. In terms of the 1978 experience because what happened here on Long Island when I came back was the following year the [district] elected me its moderator, which is its highest office, which in a way was showing support of me and kind of thumbing its nose at the denomination. So I have had very strong support from my colleagues. In seminary it would have been a little different. Those are long stories from seminary, some of which I will probably write about some day because I ran into a confrontation with the President of the seminary.

*Participant 3:* Great. As I said, there is [a couple], who are now both clergy and were very supportive. I have never had an issue with people giving me a hard time with it.

*Participant 4:* Most were not surprised. Most were disheartened that I had to resign from the roster and felt that I needed to do things to get back on the roster again. There were some who distanced themselves from me, I don't know why. I remember when I came up here to New York where my Bishop said that if I had been here you would not have had to resign. They would have dealt with the situation differently. That is one of the interesting things about [my denomination] is that while there are certain standards that are supposed to be across the whole denomination…it doesn't really work that way. Local bishops function in different sort of ways. This bishop up here is much more welcoming and affirming than the bishop was and so that's that.

*Participant 5:* I shared it with just a few who were close friends after I shared it with the leadership. Some were extremely supportive. Some were supportive of me but didn't understand it and were willing to say that. As word got out, not long after that, another woman, also, was outed at her church as a Lesbian pastor. A group of eight ministers decided they needed to get rid of the two of us. So they begin to start up witch hunts of sorts and go to talk to us. I decided from the beginning when I begin to have people question me in ways that made me feel uncomfortable that I wouldn't talk to anyone without someone else present. Of course they always did this two by two sort of in the Biblical fashion. Surprisingly they listened and for the most part didn't get, what I expected, could be very out of hand. That kind of thing. But none of those changed their minds.

I don't know if this is part of this question but we also had a process with in the denomination, in the state where I was living, where we did a common ground conference so that people could come together, ministers, to talk about this issue under the heading of Biblical authority. They made sure that they had, say, 20 people who were pro-gay and 20 who were not. Each of us were assigned to a group where there were two pro and two con. Most of the ones [conferences] that had happened before this didn't have openly gay people involved in them because they didn't know they had them in their regions. But since the two of us were known at that point, we were involved in it and one of the men who was anti-gay, was in my group, and I had known him for a long time, and basically asked me to share my story which was not on the agenda. Some of us veer from the agenda once in a while and talk about other things that they didn't tell us we could talk about. It became very meaningful for the whole group. He sort of talked about how his sister wanted to be a minister. He was sure it was the worst thing possible because he knew she was a lesbian. Therefore he was applying this same thing to me. After he heard my story and realized he had known me all these years, he decided it had less to do with his sister's sexual orientation and more about what he perceived as her not being ready or prepared or perhaps, not being fit for ministry. He almost turned the corner of being pro, not quite, but we still remain very good friends to this day.

*Participant 6:* I'll go with fellow seminarians. You know they reacted fine. I went to seminary with a partner and we were out the entire process, had a lot of support from the people of a congregation, I mean the seminarian students. I think for the most part my fellow seminarians were supportive and thought it was great in what I was doing and offered to help as much as they could. I know there were some people that were a little conservative with it. Those who may have an evangelical bent. Once they got to know me they became open and we had open discussions about it, many of them I thought were closeted gays who were struggling with it themselves. I never had anyone who was just adamant or seethingly mad about it. So, I felt the seminarian students were very supportive.

*Participant 7:* Jeez, I can't remember anybody. In our denomination it's just, "Oh."

*Participant 8:* At first, I never came out to peers. There were no peers to come out to therefore I will tell you about my Seminary peers that I came out to. When I came out in the Seminary community they were very supportive. I thought it was going to be a big deal however all the seminarians were like, "Okay, so what?" It was a big deal for me; but they didn't care. I remember the one person who I cared so much for. When I finally told [her] that I was gay she was like, "Yeah, so?" Sometimes I think coming out was a bigger deal for me than for anyone else. Eventually it became natural as fellow seminarians learned I was gay. It became a topic that wasn't an issue. It was just part of me.

Four participants reported a positive experience of coming out to laity. Participant 2 expressed how his colleagues put him up for an elected promotion as a show of their support. Participant 5 described being part of a supportive environment where the issue could be discussed. Participant 6 claimed people responded "just fine."

Two participants, 1 and 4, reported a mixed experience. Participant 1 expressed a mixed response, yet the participant only discussed the positive and supportive persons. Participant 4 voiced a sympathetic response from some while others distanced themselves.

Two participants, 7 and 8, reported a neutral experience. Both participants described an "oh" type response. The participants expressed an experience that lacked a positive or negative implication.

### Question 18: Describe how the laity reacted when you came out.

This is the final question in the attempt to understand the organizational culture's response to the coming out stage for the individual. The question rounds out a 360° examination of the organizational culture which included: supervisor/leaders, colleagues and congregations/those lead. This question attempts to get the response of those individuals which the leader was leading.

*Participant 1:* I am going to say the laity would be my church. For most of them, my coming out to them when my previous partner was diagnosed with AIDS. I came to this church, which is my first church out of seminary, with my partner. Never publicly made a statement because I was told this is how we were supposed to do it. But we moved into our apartment together. People from the church moved us into the one bedroom apartment. They included him in the life of the church but it was unspoken.

When he was diagnosed with AIDS and was getting sicker and sicker, more and more people were told because I needed to take time off. The majority of them were supportive. There were at least four people who could not support me and left. By and large they were supportive. They supported me through his death. The laity was great. They gave me time when I needed it, words of encouragement, lots of prayer support. Encouraged me afterwards and have been very accepting of my present partner. They have welcomed us as a couple. Because of the denominational stuff going on right now we have now had meetings of our board to discuss my sexuality. The consistory has met. The larger body of ruling members has met and in 1 week the congregation will meet to make sure everyone is standing firm behind me. In the event that charges are raised, we are doing this proactively to make sure the support is there. Just so everyone is aware that given what has just happened. And thus far, we have covered over 75% of the congregation; they are extremely supportive and willing to do whatever it takes to move forward. They have been great.

*Participant 2:* That has always been on a one to one basis. People ask me all the time, does the congregation that you serve know that you are gay. I would say some people know and some people do not know. I have never denied who I am; but, I have not pushed it on anyone. Sometimes it's just very natural in a conversation as we are getting to know one another and as I am revealing who I am that they come to realize that I am a gay person. That has never affected a relationship. I think the reason that it has never affected a relationship is because they have known me first. If I said this to strangers it may be quite different.

*Participant 3:* By and large good. But my denomination is very unique. I'm in a highly accepting denomination…Any G, L, B, T, Q, I, I…er…as they continue to add letters to the alphabet soup…will discover the Metropolitan Community Churches was always one of the choices for an out gay man, but if you didn't just want to be in a subculture of the gay church but wanted to be a charge that was more blended and true to life in [my denomination] is exactly where you belong. And I continue to feel that to be the case because of the high level of acceptance on behalf of lay people as well as clergy people and it has to do with education.

*Participant 4:* The bishop down there told me actually not to actually come out to them and simply resign for personal reasons. So the congregation that I had only been pastor of for 10 months never officially found out why. I just simply resigned. That was his advice.

When I moved back to [the city I previously lived in], came out to folks and there were some that were like, "Oh my god, he had been the youth pastor at this other church. I hope the kids are okay." And immediately there were other people were like saying coming on, you know this guy and he wouldn't do anything like this. It is so stupid that because you are gay they think you are going to prey on children or something. But unfortunately that is how society is.

When I came here, I was not actually, quote unquote, out to the whole congregation but there was someone who wanted to out me and I was very nervous about telling, first, my pastor-parish relations committee, then every member of the church council, then staff and other folks. All were extremely supportive. I remember one staff member saying, "You are not leaving us are you?" I said, "I am not planning on going anywhere." Folks have been extremely supportive of my ministry at this church and it is no issue that I happen to be gay. Of course, it helps that I am celibate for many of them that I honor that commitment.

*Participant 5:* Most of them were supportive to a degree. There were people who said we wished we didn't have to deal with this. But there were some who said we probably couldn't expect anything different from you but to want this to be done in honesty and integrity. I was appreciative of hearing that even if it felt backhanded at times. Some of them commented at those meetings in my home about some of my ministry with them and sort of indicated that this didn't matter. Sometimes I had the sense they were speaking to quickly. But for the most part I thought they were at least genuinely sharing that this piece was just one new piece that they were learning about me and I was learning about me and didn't really change everything. So that's, I would say, was the majority.

There were even some who so much wanted me to be kept there as their minister that one man said he had gotten me to agree to something that I had never agreed to. We had never had the conversation. I thought, "How am I going to expose this because I can't...I can't be dishonest enough to let them think that we had this conversation. And basically it had to do with how I had told him how I would never bring anyone into the parsonage without getting our approval first.

One woman, who I didn't know where she was coming from, stood up and said, "Do you think that our pastor needs to be told when to brush his teeth? Do you think he needs to be told when he should get his oil checked in his car? Do you think this?" As he said no each of those times she said, "I think I've made my point." Then he broke down and said, "I'm sorry. I don't know why I said that. The pastor and I didn't have this conversation. I just so badly wanted him to remain as our pastor that it just came out." So in a sense, he helped the integrity issue a great deal. There was so much of that. There were a lot of people who said, "We love you but..." and "Here is the 800 number to call." It was just those few, there were very few, that were what I call mean-spirited.

*Participant 6:* There again, I'll take the parish where I was sponsored as a...for [the ministry]...as a candidate for [the ministry]. I have been out with that parish since the get go. There assistant [minister] was gay and open and there were several gay couples and several single gay people. During the process while I was there a lesbian came to Christ through the Catechumen process and was baptized at an Easter vigil. So it's not really a matter of me coming out with them...it was just I was never not out with them. And still that parish supported me for going to seminary.

*Participant 7:* Again that presumes that coming out is a single event. I did not tell laity. They simply either knew before I went to that church or found out. At no point have I been made to feel uncomfortable or unwelcome because of my sexuality.

*Participant 8:* I never came out to laity. By the time I came out I was serving a gay and lesbian congregation. There is not much of an issue in coming out there. They kinda know from the get-go.

Two participants told the laity as a group. Participant 1 came out to his parish in a time of crisis (the loss of his partner). Participant 5 came out to his parish in several groups of the laity at meetings.

Four participants reported they have served as an openly gay minister, therefore, negating the need to come out to the laity. Participants 3 and 6 reported being in a denomination that would allow him to always be open. Participant 7 reported that he has never went to a church that didn't know; however, he does not provide the means which they find out. He only informed us they simply knew or found out. Participant 8 reported in serving openly since coming out.

Four participants reported some form of positive support through the process of coming out to the laity. Participant 1 reported, in detail, the crisis of losing his partner and the support the laity provided. Participant 5 reported a majority of people being supportive. Participants 6 and 7 provided a simple supportive statement.

## Question 19: Have any of these persons' reactions changed over time and if so how?

This question attempts to examine if there is a process occurring over time from when the individual came out to present. The question gears the participants to focus on whether the individuals have changed, however, and more importantly, has the organizational culture as reflected through these people changed.

*Participant 1:* For some of them, yeah. Their reactions for some of them at first were unsure. A few of them shared that from in theory and their study of the scripture this is wrong, but knowing their pastor and having had their pastor work with them through various issues they have really had to look at the question. For some of them it has been a real movement from this is what the bible says, homosexuality is wrong, sinful to this is our pastor, God has gifted him and he's been used by God…let's look at what the scripture say. Let's take another look at that. For some of them it has been a difficult journey. Some of them are further along. There are still a few who aren't sure. They are accepting of their gay pastor but they are not sure if they are ready to embrace all gay, lesbian, transgender, and bisexuals. Not quite ready to go there, some of them.

*Participant 2:* Well, going back to 1978 there were a couple people who were going to vote against ordination of gay and lesbians, that after I told my story reversed their vote. One of them, an elder from Massapequa, said, "I thought I had this thing already worked out but now I have to deal with you." It was beautiful. He gave me a big hug when he said that. He and his wife, and later his daughter, became very outspoken in terms of the rights of gays and lesbians within our denomination. So a real turn about for him.

*Participant 3:* No. Parents may be are the only but that is beyond peers or clergy colleagues. Because I had basically been out before most of these people know me. I moved around so much and I was very much out throughout my seminary in my first couple churches and now my third church. So I don't have the benefit of the before and after.

*Participant 4:* The folks in Miami who initially were concerned with the kids, their reactions have changed when they realized that their initial reaction was a little unfounded. In fact, one couple that has said that has come to visit me here in New York. We are good friends. We were before. Folks here in New York, they just continue to be supportive of me and my ministry. And in fact, are beginning to be more supportive of gays and lesbians in the congregation who have either been there and have become more prevalent or have come to the congregation since I have been there. I don't know if my presence has brought them there but I think they might see it a bit more welcoming since there is a gay pastor.

*Participant 5:* I don't know that I would say they have changed, but I think the ones who accepted me and didn't want to dissociate from me and didn't understand at all have remained friends and colleagues. They have not...not kind of...not turned away. One of the people was an executive who came after the other one left. He had not been...he had not understood it but we had known each other for such a long time and even as an executive who kind of rides the fence, I feel that if I ask him to advocate for me, he would. Because he knows me.

*Participant 6:* No, not at all. Of course you know that was many years ago. It's probably 10 or 15 years ago when I was in that congregation going through that process and I have lost touch with a lot of them but they continue to be supportive. Some members from that congregation came to when I was installed at the rector here. That congregation made a stole, a Diaconal Stole, when I was ordained a deacon. So the support continued all along.

*Participant 7:* Not that I am aware of.

*Participant 8:* A colleague and fellow minister of mine has come along ways with the issue. They went from being an ultra conservative to now their friend is gay. I became the face of an issue that was abhorrent to him. He didn't reject me straight out; however, he allowed himself to explore the issue. He went and took a course at the local college on human sexuality. I was so proud of him. I think our relationship has grown stronger as I have seen him grow and accept me.

Four participants reported no change in the individuals previously discussed after the coming out process and present. Participant 3 explained most people knew he was out since they have known him so there was no opportunity for change. Participant 5 said those who accepted him then have continued to do so. Participants 6 and 7 each reported simply no known changes.

Four participants reported a change. Participant 1 reported an "unsure" reaction that later turned to an acceptance, in spite they could not work it out biblically. Participant 2 reported a change in a district vote after sharing his story. Participant 4 reported a concern being voiced about the children the minister worked with and later the individuals who made these issues dismissed them. Participant 4 reported moving all the way to a friendship. Participant 8 specifically talked of an individual's theological movement by knowing the participant.

## Question 20: How do you reconcile, as a religious leader, the organizational culture of your denomination and your sexual orientation?

The final two questions focus on the integration stage of the coming out process. This question seeks to address the reconciliation of the organizational culture and the individual.

*Participant 1:* Used to be by ignoring them. Just kind of going on in my congregation. The executive from our denomination who approached me when I was getting ready to leave asked me to become [a district position] which pulled me into the denomination. Prior to that, I kept a low profile. What that has done is helped me to see how to work within to make people aware of concerns of gay and lesbians and also I think in many cases to put a face on it. Knowing ultimately, this is something that is hanging there, that any time charges could be raised that would stir up a controversy which ultimately after a process could lead to my removal. It is kind of exciting to be a part of that but also knowing that by stepping out and being more vocal that it increases that risk. But my congregation is behind me.

*Participant 2:* Well, in most cases, the moderator of our general assembly has been very open with gay and lesbians; but, he has had to deal with a very strong element within the denomination that does not approve. I guess that I have been able to get by because I am well liked where I am. I might have real difficulty should I transfer to a different [district]. If I moved out of this area and went to another state. I may have real difficulty because each [district], each local [district], can re-examine you and can ask you any question they want to. I am very much safe here.

*Participant 3:* There is no reconciliation needed.

*Participant 4:* Well, our denomination is struggling with that. This summer at the national assembly they will vote on whether to allow gays and lesbians to have a holy union or something like that and then also whether to allow gays and lesbians in committed relationships to be active in the ordained ministry. They already are but to make it official thing. We are not sure where it is going to come down on that. I have a feeling in my gut that it is going to be what is called the local option which means different bishops will deal with things differently. Our bishop knows that there are people in committed relationships who are in congregations in leadership positions, even on his own staff. He is very supportive and caring. Sometimes he has to walk a fine line and turn a blind eye type thing but he is very supportive of us. He is very supportive of me. So I don't see there is going to be a problem or anything.

*Participant 5:* I think sometimes its easier being a [my denomination] to do that than in some denominations. I have worked, since I came out, I guess first I should go back and say that I really thought there would be a lot of a resentment for someone coming out at a late age. Where were you when we were going through all this stuff from our 20s on up. It wasn't like that at all. They welcomed me. They welcomed someone who finally figured it out, I guess you could say. I then began to work both nationally and locally with our affirming movement. Because of that, really knew what was really going on in all respects.

I guess I began to appreciate what it meant to be a [my denomination], even more. Most of the positive things that happened within churches with the laity and with colleagues and with people in the denomination really...really in the best since of the word arrived at the conclusions at well this may be all right for you and your church but it doesn't have to be for us. Hopefully, vice versa, that any objections they might have doesn't necessarily have to cause a church that I serve to change the way they do things. They do it through the association principle, voluntary association. We listen to people. We listen to associations. We listen to what's going on and how people feel about it.

*Participant 6:* Well, I think...I don't have any problem reconciling it. I think what's going on with...I think gays and lesbians have always been active people in the church. They have had to hide it because it is some sort of sexual taboo. Although I think that's a real poor interpretation and understanding of Scripture. And I think [my denomination] has come to that point where they understand that many of the traditional moral stands, if you will call the moral stands, on sexuality were very much the product of the culture of the time, from the early church or from the early times Christianity. As an example, [my denomination] while still maintaining its Catholicity, as being a Catholic denomination, a reformed Catholic denomination, came to the decision in 1979 that being a woman can really be no bar to being [a minister]. That in our overall understanding of Christ and his message that there is no male or female. That was just not an argument that holds up. The fact that Jesus had male disciples, well Jesus also had Mary Magdalene, his mother hanging around, and his other Mary's. And also the women were the first apostles. They were the first ones who bore the news of the resurrection. So to refuse them ordination because of sort of cultural circumstances or relationships between men and women just didn't hold water anymore. In the same way that is how we're dealing with the issues of sexuality, looking at the verses of the Bible that refer to homosexuality, putting them in cultural context, and realizing that in many ways those cultural contexts do not apply to the current situation of people trying to develop loving relationships even raising families and trying to build a life together. And so, they're looking at that any kind of a new…a new light. If we believe the Church is guided by the Holy Spirit into all truth, then that would make perfect sense. We can't believe that all the spirit's truth was revealed in the first 200 years of the church and then that was it. Otherwise, then it's dead. It's a dead religion. And I think that's how [my denomination] is looking at. [My denomination] is making great strides however we're still dealing with a wider [denominational] communion in other cultures, primarily African cultures and Asian cultures, which haven't really come to the terms of the role of the proper place of women. In fact to raise it to another level to deal with human sexuality they are just not in that place yet. So that's causing conflict. But we're doing a lot of work with dialogue between the first world and third world countries and trying to come to some understanding and focus on the positives. I don't off I answer that question but...[laughs].

*Participant 7:* Well, I have the good fortune of having been born into this denomination. So it is not a problem.

*Participant 8:* I don't reconcile with my former organizational culture. I believe they are uneducated and ignorant. There is little that I can do to reconcile with them. Instead, I have found a church that will accept me and that I can accept them.

Four participants reported organizational cultures that allowed a local reconciliation; however, there was no larger organizational reconciliation available to them. Participants 1, 2, and 5 each reported a denomination that is struggling with this issue. While these three participants were accepted at their local congregation and perhaps district level, each voiced the understanding they may not be able to leave their individual church or district. Participant 6 discussed the issue in the larger church. Participant 6 explained that while his denomination had reconciled the issue in the United States, there were factions across the world that did not agree.

Four participants reported there was no need for reconciliation. They were part of a denomination that accepted them fully and therefore, additional reconciliation was not needed.

One participant claimed he had not reconciled. Participant 8 reported outside the interview that he had changed denominations to a congregation that did not require reconciliation. Therefore, while he is reconciled in his current church, there was no reconciliation with the previous organizational culture.

### Question 21: How has accepting your own sexual orientation affected your development as a religious leader?

The final question in the interview, continuing with the integration stage themed questions, asks the participant to reflect upon this process's influence on their life. It seeks to examine how this process has affected their organizational culture leadership.

*Participant 1:* One of the things that it helps me to bring to my pastoral work is that I am very sensitive to people's need for acceptance and respect...inclusion. It has really helped me in my ministry to develop a real sense of the power of God's love and to focus on that, and to stress the importance of living that out that it embraces all people. My congregation, I think, has been enriched by the fact that I bring to my ministry as a gay person a real awareness of what it means to be on the outside looking in, not fully apart of things. It has helped many of them who have felt for whatever reason in their own lives that they are not part of a situation that here they have a place. I think it also has made me more attuned to what people are saying, behind what the words are. One of the things, I think, that many of us who are gay or lesbian learn early on is how to read people because we are so careful and protective, especially when we are young. And I think that is a real gift to bring to people in a ministry, to be able to really be there with them.

*Participant 2:* Well, I think that because of everything I have been through I am able to listen to people's story and resonate with what they have gone through. Although I have never in listening to somebody tell their story tell them I understand. I realize that their story is their story. Should I ever say I understand, I am no longer listening to their story, I am hearing my own again. So that has been a key thing in doing any counseling work. To really let that other person tell their story. Let me give you a concrete example. A few years ago a female pastor referred a female member of her congregation to me. She did not feel comfortable with this person who identified herself as a lesbian. This person called me and wanted to know if she could meet with me. She said I understand that you would be open to talking with someone who is a lesbian. I met with this person three times before I came to realize that although she described herself as a lesbian that she had never been physically involved with another woman. I had to realize then that because of the terms she used that I had come to certain conclusions which I had eliminated. Thank goodness I never said that to her.

*Participant 3:* He gave me kind of a unique focus when it came down to time to have to come up with a focus for my...we didn't call it a dissertation...my final project in seminary...my senior project or whatever they call it. I did it on how same sex couples celebrate their relationships in the form of marriage. How do you marry, liturgically? Why and what does it look like? This was 1991. That was my focus in seminary. So it allowed me to put together and I was going to publish a book and I still have all my research and everything all done. I should probably turn it into a book because in today's reality it would probably be quite helpful. Suggestions language to use, how do you decide what language to use. Do you call the person a partner, a wife, a husband? Is the covenant told relationship that you're celebrating...do you call it a marriage? What is it that you're doing? Gets into the language of that. They gave me that focus, and it allowed me to learn a great deal about a topic that has proven to be quite recently timely to my benefit.

*Participant 4:* Very much so. I think my theology has always been centered around self-esteem and the fact that we are loved unconditionally by God. As I have moved beyond that internal homophobia to an appreciation of who I am and who's I am, I think that has made me a much more effective pastor. I am willing to take risk more. I am willing to be honest with who I am. I am more open to different attitudes and things that different people have. Having gone through this process of going off the roster and being put back on the roster again, I don't take myself so seriously anymore. I am able to laugh at things and at my foibles and things like that. I think it has changed my ministry dramatically for the better.

*Participant 5:* I guess personally I think it was immense because that's why I went back to what the person said about my life becoming more whole. I think I was always somewhat confident within, but I grew up very much an introvert and had to make myself an extrovert in some of the things I did. I guess I felt, like sometimes we say that you find your voice that you haven't had as you experience crisis in life or some point of your journey takes you to this place or that. It's just been a much more fulfilling life as far as being a minister and being apart of the denomination. I think there has been more respect for me because I haven't...haven't backed down from them. I have never felt I needed to hide it and let people think that it really wasn't a part of who I am, because it was just a strong part of who I am.

*Participant 6:* It's been great. To me it's a matter of integrity honesty and truth. That's what I try to teach people as being part of the gospel. I think we can't be healed or touched by God...by Jesus and God, if we are trying to hide part of ourselves from God. There's nothing so horrible that God can't love us and want to help us grow. That's why often times when I teach, I talk about people doing confession because...when I say things that are like horrible enough, I am not talking about homosexuality, and just talking about anything that people do. Whether it's cheating at work or being nasty with people or something...there's nothing we can do but we have to come to terms with it. Part of the message is being honest with ourselves and confessing those in the guide can help us to grow and to heal and to forgive us of those. But if we hide them, even though I don't think God...nothing is really hidden from God. But I think God allows us to hide things from him if we feel we want to. That breaks up the relationship that we have between God and ourselves. So for me the entire thing of dealing with my sexuality, coming to terms with it, being honest with it is a matter of integrity, honesty, and truth. I feel that the truth will set you free. It's difficult and times, but I don't think there's anything else we can do. Not only as an ordained person but as a baptized Christian.

*Participant 7:* I don't think there is any question that I made choices early on vocationally that reflected my own anxiety about the acceptability of my sexual feelings. I chose to remain in New York City when I had opportunities to go to larger churches outside of New York City. I chose another career. I am a psychologist, as well as, a minister, thinking that there probably was not much future for me in the church. But that was not because of my sexuality. That was because my first 12 years experience was in a very politically active, dynamic, radicalized church community that was going to be very hard to find anywhere else but could not afford to support me, 3 kids and the wife very well. So I looked for other career possibilities.

I am sure that I wouldn't say my coming out but I would say my awareness of my own sexuality has always made me empathic with others who are seen as outcast or marginalized. I was very involved with civil rights activities of various kinds those years. So I would say that my ministry always had a strong social action bent in part, but only in part, because of my sexual orientation.

*Participant 8:* It has required me to think out of the box. Things don't work the traditional way for a gay pastor, or at least not for me. I had to make my own educational plans, my own ordination plans, and my own life plans. There was no fixed system for me to appeal to. It made me a stronger person who learned to think outside the box. I had to become better at managing what I wanted and how I would get it. Things were not always easily available for a gay clergy. Some congregations do not want a gay man for a minister. Therefore options become limited and the process becomes more selective.

Another thing it that my theology has changed considerably. I went from a fundamental theology where I was obligated to certain behavior to a liberal theology where I was liberated to be. It may sound corny but you move away from the emotional touch of spirituality to a very logical and intellectual spirituality.

Seven participants addressed this question including their ability they have to relate to others. Words were utilized such as "acceptance" and "inclusion." Participants 1, 2, and 6 gave illustrations of how their ability to think inclusively has developed. Participants 4 and 7 included their ability to be empathic or love people.

# Qualitative Analysis of the Text Data

In keeping with the conceptualization of Moustakas (1990), the text of the interviews were then read and re-read several times by the researcher. Excerpts of the interviews were extrapolated to in this process that outlined several themes that were common through the interviews. These themes shed light onto our earlier proposed research questions.

### Don't Ask, Don't Tell

The first theme that emerges is the concept of a don't ask, don't tell organizational culture. When one attempts to review the level of support an organizational culture maintains, then one must examine two aspects: supervisors and organizational positions and members and colleagues. The don't ask, don't tell policy was a theme that existed in the supervisors and organizational positions. Individual accounts are filled with statements of support and fear of repercussions. A fine line is navigated in the minister's life between being out and being an activist, being out and being overexposed, and being out and maintaining denominational compliance.

### Participant 1 Meaning Units.

1. Since I have been in it [my denomination], the official policy [on homosexuality] has been opposed.

2. In practice it's don't ask, don't tell.

3. The organizational structure/system always has said that as long as you remain quiet it is okay.

4. The church was the last place I came out.

5. I came to this church, which is my first church out of seminary, with my partner. Never publicly made a statement because I was told this is how we were supposed to do it.

### Participant 2 Meaning Units.

1. Well, I grew up in a very conservative church so though it wasn't spelled out directly, any sexual activity was frowned upon.

2. Well, like I said, there was prohibition on sexual activity outside of marriage, so that was so frowned on that certainly my sexual activity, I saw to be frowned upon as well.

3. I don't think I ever really talked to anybody about it.

4. Well, in most cases, the moderator of our general assembly has been very open with gay and lesbians; but, he has had to deal with a very strong element within the denomination that does not approve.

### Participant 4 Meaning Units.

1. However, the idea was that gays and lesbians were welcomed into the community and certainly gays and lesbians could serve in the ordained ministry, but they must remain celibate.

2.   I was in a relationship with a person [locally] and the bishops sent [a denominational official] and another person to talk to me because members of the congregation had suspected that I was gay, they didn't know necessarily that I was in a relationship but suspected that I was gay, and so they wanted me to talk to them about that.

3.   Though folks may have suspected that I was gay because I was getting older and was single and not dating anybody those issues never came up as a question.

4.   The bishop required me to resign from the roster because I was not in compliance that says that gay and lesbian pastors must remain celibate.

5.   I think at the time sadness because I knew how wonderful the relationship was and how sad it was that this could not be shared openly with other people.

6.   That is one of the interesting things about [my denomination] is that while there are certain standards that are supposed to be across the whole denomination…it doesn't really work that way.

7.   The bishop down there told me actually not to actually come out to them and simply resign for personal reasons.

### Participant 5 Meaning Units.

1.   There were times as I was ministering and growing up and so on that, I think there was an openness because people understood that our denominational polity means churches can decide for themselves.

2.   They began to try to present resolutions and other kind of things that would limit any involvement of homosexuals with the denomination.

3. I decided that I didn't want any denominational persons, other than those few people at the church who knew and promised to keep their mouth shut to know anything, especially the leadership.

4. Sometimes he [supervisor] has to walk a fine line and turn a blind eye type thing but he is very supportive of us.

*Participant 6 Meaning Units.*

1. Basically, my denomination has already resolved that being gay or lesbian is not a bar to being ordained or participating fully in the life of the church. Currently in the worldwide [denominational community] that's causing a lot of riff.

2. They [the denomination] have struggled with trying to accept that [homosexuality] and to be more open with that and to be more affirming of that although they came along way.

*Participant 7 Meaning Units.*

1. So the culture has shifted very rapidly from ignoring the subject to being, at least verbally, very open.

*Participant 8 Meaning Units.*

1. I lost my church, I was kicked out of college, one of the denominational people said he heard a rumor that I was faggot and they didn't want a faggot walking around with a degree from their school.

## Local Supportive Organizational Cultures

While the organizational policies and direct supervisors may adopt a don't ask, don't tell policy, the local organizational culture, where the minister works on a daily basis, tends to be much more supportive. The participants report a strong supportive culture of congregational members and colleagues.

### Participant 1 Meaning Units.

1.   He [Denominational leader] includes us as a couple, regularly in all denominational functions. It is great.

2.   But overall, I would have to say that during that time the seminary was really accepting as were my professors.

3.   Peers were great.

4.   People from the church moved us into the one bedroom apartment. They included him in the life of the church but it was unspoken.

5.   When he was diagnosed with AIDS and was getting sicker and sicker, more and more people were told because I needed to take time off. The majority of them were supportive.

6.   By and large they [the congregation] were supportive.

7.   They supported me through his death.

8.   The laity was great.

9.   The larger body of ruling members has met and in 1 week the congregation will meet to make sure everyone is standing firm behind me. In the event that charges are raised, we are doing this proactively to make sure the support is there. Just so everyone is aware that given what has just happened. And thus far, we have covered over 75% of the congregation; they are extremely supportive and willing to do whatever it takes to move forward. They have been great.

10.   They are accepting of their gay pastor but they are not sure if they are ready to embrace all gay, lesbian, transgender, and bisexuals.

### Participant 2 Meaning Units.

1. When I was in seminary, I was very open about my homosexuality. It caused no problem within the seminary....

2. Then in every case they [colleagues] came up in embraced me.

3. One woman who I had always thought of to be very conservative in her theology. She came from the south. She came up to me she used language that I am sure she never used before. She said, "I was wondering how long you were going to take this shit." Then gave me a big kiss.

4. The following year the [district] elected me its moderator, which is its highest office, which in a way was showing support of me and kind of thumbing its nose at the denomination.

5. Sometimes it's just very natural in a conversation as we are getting to know one another and as I am revealing who I am that they come to realize that I am a gay person. That has never affected a relationship.

### Participant 3 Meaning Units.

1. I have never had an issue with people giving me a hard time with it.

2. And I continue to feel that to be the case because of the high level of acceptance on behalf of lay people as well as clergy people and it has to do with education.

### Participant 4 Meaning Units.

1. Shortly thereafter, one of the other [denominational] pastors needed a parish administrator. He said he felt it was a crime the way the church had treated me because of having to resign cause he knew I was a good pastor.

2.  So that sense of warmth, of people in my denomination who knew me as a person, accepted me, it was a very powerful experience.

3.  What a joy it was to know that yes in my denomination while the official policy maybe that I couldn't be in a committed relationship and be a pastor, that I can function as a pastor and eventually work back into being able to preach and preside in [my denomination] again.

4.  Most were disheartened that I had to resign from the roster and felt that I needed to do things to get back on the roster again.

5.  I was very nervous about telling, first, my pastor-parish relations committee, then every member of the church council, then staff and other folks. All were extremely supportive.

6.  Folks have been extremely supportive of my ministry at this church and it is no issue that I happen to be gay.

7.  Folks here in New York, they just continue to be supportive of me and my ministry.

### *Participant 5 Meaning Units.*

1.  I've always been very fortunate to have good relationships with the people in the church.

2.  They have always appreciated the ministry that I brought, found me to be pastoral....

3.  But in the process decided that I needed to talk to them [members of his church] because I did trust them.

4.  I felt they would do well by me whether it meant its time to give up your family, your church, your life.

5.  At least I knew they would be fair people and they were.

6. They [the church] basically recommended that I be affirmed as a person and as their minister and kept as their pastor.

7. Some were extremely supportive. Some were supportive of me but didn't understand it and were willing to say that.

8. But for the most part I thought they were at least genuinely sharing that this piece was just one new piece that they were learning about me and I was learning about me and didn't really change everything.

### *Participant 6 Meaning Units.*

1. Mostly through church met other people who introduced me to the gay culture and found out it wasn't really anything to be afraid of and actually I fit in very well and was comfortable there.

2. You know they [colleagues] reacted fine.

3. I went to seminary with a partner and we were out the entire process, had a lot of support from the people of a congregation, I mean the seminarian students.

4. I think for the most part my fellow seminarians were supportive and thought it was great in what I was doing and offered to help as much as they could.

5. So it's not really a matter of me coming out with them...it was just I was never not out with them. And still that parish supported me for going to seminary.

6. Some members from that congregation came to when I was installed at the rector here. That congregation made a stole, a Diaconal Stole, when I was ordained a deacon. So the support continued all along.

### *Participant 7 Meaning Units.*

1. I had colleagues that were gay.

2.  I suppose the first time I went to [the national conference of my denomination] and participated as an openly gay man with a boyfriend.

3.  I did not tell laity. They simply either knew before I went to that church or found out. At no point have I been made to feel uncomfortable or unwelcome because of my sexuality.

### Participant 8 Meaning Units.

1.  When I came out in the Seminary community they were very supportive.

2.  Sometimes I think coming out was a bigger deal for me than for anyone else. Eventually it became natural as fellow seminarians learned I was gay. It became a topic that wasn't an issue. It was just part of me.

3.  A colleague and fellow minister of mine has come along ways with the issue. They went from being an ultra conservative to now their friend is gay. I became the face of an issue that was abhorrent to him. He didn't reject me straight out; however, he allowed himself to explore the issue. He went and took a course at the local college on human sexuality. I was so proud of him. I think our relationship has grown stronger as I have seen him grow and accept me.

## Importance of Relational Leadership

Another common theme that appeared in all participants was the emphasis placed on relational leadership. There are several references to the leader's integrity and honesty and its impact on the individuals around them within the organizational culture. The participants referred to their careers and leadership impact on others as being asked to take denominational leadership positions, characterized by comments of integrity and honesty, with followers making comments about their impact, and theological and philosophical ideological transformations. They may be gay; however, they are men of honesty and integrity who impact those they lead by their individual life.

### Participant 1 Meaning Units.

1. A few of them shared that from in theory and their study of the scripture this is wrong, but knowing their pastor and having had their pastor work with them through various issues they have really had to look at the question.

2. For some of them it has been a real movement from this is what the bible says, homosexuality is wrong, sinful to this is our pastor, God has gifted him and he's been used by God...let's look at what the scripture say. Let's take another look at that.

3. They are accepting of their gay pastor but they are not sure if they are ready to embrace all gay, lesbian, transgender, and bisexuals.

4. The executive from our denomination who approached me when I was getting ready to leave asked me to become the [district position] which pulled me into the denomination.

5. Knowing ultimately, this is something that is hanging there, that any time charges could be raised that would stir up a controversy which ultimately after a process could lead to my removal...But my congregation is behind me.

6. My congregation, I think, has been enriched by the fact that I bring to my ministry as a gay person a real awareness of what it means to be on the outside looking in, not fully apart of things.

7. It has helped many of them who have felt for whatever reason in their own lives that they are not part of a situation that here they have a place.

### Participant 2 Meaning Units.

1. People knew that I had already made a real contribution to the denomination.

2. In terms of the 1978 experience, because what happened here on Long Island, when I came back was the following year the [district] elected me its moderator, which is its highest office....

3. I guess that I have been able to get by because I am well liked where I am.

4. I am very much safe here.

### Participant 4 Meaning Units.

1. Able to rise through the ranks, very much respected, able to get calls easily.

2. I was able to get calls without any problems whatsoever....

3. I was able to be involved in leadership positions beyond the congregation, in what is the district what we call the [district] and even in the national church.

4. He said he felt it was a crime the way the church had treated me because of having to resign cause he knew I was a good pastor.

5. My former bishop, who was retired at the time, the bishop who ordained me said that the church was losing one of its greatest pastors.

6. Most were disheartened that I had to resign from the roster and felt that I needed to do things to get back on the roster again.

7. I remember one staff member saying, "You are not leaving us are you?"

### Participant 5 Meaning Units.

1. But there were some who said we probably couldn't expect anything different from you but to want this to be done in honesty and integrity.

2. I thought, "How am I going to expose this because I can't...I can't be dishonest enough to let them think that we had this conversation."

3. I just so badly wanted him to remain as our pastor....

4. One of the people was an executive who came after the other one left. He had not been...he had not understood it but we had known each other for such a long time and even as an executive who kind of rides the fence, I feel that if I ask him to advocate for me, he would. Because he knows me.

5. I think there has been more respect for me because I haven't...haven't backed down from them.

### Participant 6 Meaning Units.

1. To me it's a matter of integrity honesty and truth.

2. I think we can't be healed or touched by God...by Jesus and God, if we are trying to hide part of ourselves from God.

3. So for me the entire thing of dealing with my sexuality, coming to terms with it, being honest with it is a matter of integrity, honesty, and truth.

4. I feel that the truth will set you free.

### Participant 7 Meaning Units.

1. One of them was a vibrant inner-city church that flourished under my leadership.

2.    I started being appointed to committees as clearly the openly gay representative.

### Participant 8 Meaning Units.

1.    I worked for the denomination on a lot of things.

## Long-Term Relationship to the Organizational Culture

One of the common elements that remain consistent with the participants is a history of high levels of activity in relating to the culture. There is a great amount of involvement and interaction, prior to serving as clergy, with the culture of the organization. This involvement may include growing up, schools, and colleges.

### Participant 1 Meaning Units.

1.    I went to a denominational college....

### Participant 2 Meaning Units.

1.    I grew up in a very conservative church....

2.    The high school that I went to...was a church related high school.

3.    Well, in high school there was some tension in terms of getting involved and feeling real guilt about it. Praying and asking for forgiveness and I would never get involved again.

### Participant 3 Meaning Units.

1.    I worked for Christian ministry at the National Parks, so I was very involved with church and fellowship and that kind of stuff and was not out with them.

2.    They asked me to pastor while I was there so for those 3 months while I was there during the harvest, I preached there for them.

3.  Then I worked for Covenant Players of Christian Ministry for theater Ministry and I wasn't really out doing that but it was itinerant Ministry visiting different churches.

4.  When I was first year in seminary, I went to work for the national offices of my denomination. I was a member of [a local] church. As a [church member], I would regularly attend with [my partner]. I got very active in that church.

5.  We had a really cool and very intelligent Protestant campus minister, full-time also professor. He was great. So I got involved there....

### *Participant 4 Meaning Units.*

1.  Because my understanding of things was that I really understood from a very early age that I wanted to be a pastor....

2.  It was painful because in the coming out I had to resign from being a pastor which is what I wanted to do for my entire life.

### *Participant 5 Meaning Units.*

1.  I started involvement in the church at the second grade level and stayed with it.

2.  I did church camp over the years.

3.  I went to a [denominational] related college, [denominational] seminary....

4.  There were times as I was...growing up and so on that, I think there was an openness because people understood that our denominational polity means churches can decide for themselves.

5.  I've always been very fortunate to have good relationships with the people in the church.

### Participant 6 Meaning Units.

1. I have been actively involved in the church for most of my adulthood starting when I was about 21....

2. I have always had a good relationship with the church.

3. I was one of those kids who was always active in youth group and loved serving at the altar as a server.

4. And had thought about seminary actually since I was a very young person, probably around 10 or so.

5. Mostly through church met other people who introduced me to the gay culture and found out it wasn't really anything to be afraid of and actually I fit in very well and was comfortable there.

### Participant 8 Meaning Units.

1. I was very active.

2. All of my spare time was spent in activities of the church.

3. I missed my prom in high school because I was doing something for the church.

4. I was a youth leader, lay leader, and then went on immediately to become a minister.

5. I told my parents when I was 12 years old that I wanted to be a minister.

## Empathy and Inclusiveness with Others

The participants had a theme of empathy and inclusiveness with others. As a direct response of their coming out process, the participants claimed to have an increased ability to relate to others by utilizing comments of acceptance, inclusion, empathy, and love. The coming out process is accredited by the participants for these compassionate responses. This behavior is attributed to be a direct response of the coming out process on their interaction with the organizational culture.

### Participant 1 Meaning Units.

1. One of the things that it helps me to bring to my pastoral work is that I am very sensitive to people's need for acceptance and respect...inclusion.

2. My congregation, I think, has been enriched by the fact that I bring to my ministry as a gay person a real awareness of what it means to be on the outside looking in, not fully apart of things.

3. I think it also has made me more attuned to what people are saying, behind what the words are.

4. One of the things, I think, that many of us who are gay or lesbian learn early on is how to read people because we are so careful and protective, especially when we are young.

### Participant 2 Meaning Units.

1. Well, I think that because of everything I have been through I am able to listen to people's story and resonate with what they have gone through.

### Participant 4 Meaning Units.

1. I think my theology has always been centered around self-esteem and the fact that we are loved unconditionally by God.

2. I am more open to different attitudes and things that different people have.

### Participant 5 Meaning Units.

1.  We listen to people. We listen to associations. We listen to what's going on and how people feel about it.

### Participant 7 Meaning Units.

1.  I am sure that I wouldn't say my coming out but I would say my awareness of my own sexuality has always made me empathic with others who are seen as outcast or marginalized.

## Sense of Duality Between Organizational Culture and Psychosexual Development

The participants often adhere to a sense of a duality theme between their organizational culture and their psychosexual developmental needs. While this dynamic may be described as a theological/professional role and psychosexual role, the duality of needs are expressed as not being fully met by the organizational culture. The psychosexual development is never fully embraced within the organizational culture and therefore leaves the participants reporting needs to fulfill wholeness and their inclusivity from exterior sources. These statements, directly or indirectly, address the issue of the dual influences/roles that are struggled with.

### Participant 1 Meaning Units.

1.  It was liberating, freeing…exciting in many ways for me to be apart of where I felt accepted and where I felt that who I was…was actually valued.

2.  Just surrounded in a culture that I felt this was great this is where I want to be.

3.  One of the things that it helps me to bring to my pastoral work is that I am very sensitive to people's need for acceptance and respect…inclusion.

### Participant 2 Meaning Units.

1. We are going to go where we are accepted.

2. More recently, it means they have gotten ordained or if they are already ordained they are transferred to [another denomination] where there is a more open policy.

3. I said thanks a lot; you didn't ask me how I feel or anything like that.

### Participant 3 Meaning Units.

1. With him I went to the gay bars and realized there was more than a sex culture.

2. I didn't realize there is real life.

3. It was sort of surprising and it was a wonderful awakening on a lot of levels and met lots of good people who are friends of [my partner].

### Participant 4 Meaning Units.

1. Then, as I got closer to that age, 35 or whatever it was, there was almost a dual life that I was living the life of a pastor where folks didn't know I was gay as a matter fact people were surprised to find out I was gay.

2. Because it was hard to constantly have to change the pronouns and all the other kind of stuff like many of us have had to do…to talk about her instead of really saying it's him and play those type of things.

3. Well, actually I first experienced the gay culture most and got rid of the internal homophobia when I was off the roster of my denomination.

4. They [A local MCC Church] really taught me through bible studies and through other things…how to learn to love

myself, and that being gay was a gift from God, and it wasn't something I needed to beat myself up about and that one could be gay and a faithful Pastor at the same time.

5.   There was not a deeper level of relationship, the appreciation that two men can be caring for each other in a way that I had experienced with my parents, who are heterosexual, in the way they cared for each other and were involved in each others lives beyond casual relationships.

6.   So I would say the relationship with my partner was a first, it was quite unique and gratifying that to know that a relationship could be more than a sexual encounter.

7.   I think at the time sadness because I knew how wonderful the relationship was and how sad it was that this could not be shared openly with other people.

8.   And how sad it was that people could not appreciate the kind of relationship that God creates or desires for us to have, a life long relationship, just because it happens to be with gay people, me in this particular circumstance, that this could not be rejoiced and celebrated as much as when heterosexual people get together.

9.   Ended up moving back to [city name deleted] to a community that was more supportive.

10.  So that sense of warmth, of people in my denomination who knew me as a person, accepted me, it was a very powerful experience.

11.  So there was the pain and a sense of loss, but eventually a sense of joy that I could be accepted for who I am and be able to be a pastor.

12. I think my theology has always been centered around self-esteem and the fact that we are loved unconditionally by God.

### Participant 5 Meaning Units.

1. I was living a lie and didn't know it.

2. They put me in touch with someone who had come out at a later age and we both kind of sat there and talked about the why me, why now kind of thing.

3. But I did begin to go to bars because those were the only places to go to meet people.

4. But, it was a real learning thing and I felt I had to be there to be with people who were like myself because for most of the week I was with primarily heterosexual people and I needed to figure out what this was all about.

5. But at that point felt I needed to connect with people who were maybe more like me.

6. I had the feeling that they did accept and they knew was much more than just this one new piece of information.

### Participant 6 Meaning Units.

1. Mostly through church met other people who introduced me to the gay culture and found out it wasn't really anything to be afraid of and actually I fit in very well and was comfortable there.

### Participant 7 Meaning Units.

1. At some point between seminary and the first few years of my ministry I became aware that there was much more gay life than I had been aware of growing up, but it was just part of the ambiance of New York.

2.    I thought of my church as progressive, welcoming, exciting.

***Participant 8 Meaning Units.***

1.    There is a feeling of complete isolation and abandonment as you have to carry this experience all alone.

2.    Instead, I have found a church that will accept me and that I can accept them.

# Summary

Based upon the responses provided, the organizational cultures can be divided into three distinct types in respect to the organizational position on homosexuality: open and accepting, qualified acceptance, and absolute condemnation (see Table 6). Three participants describe their organizational culture as open and affirming. Three participants describe their organizational culture as qualified acceptance. Two describe their organizational cultures as absolute condemnation.

### Table 6. Organizational Culture Responses

| Response | Description |
| --- | --- |
| Open and accepting | The organizational culture promotes complete acceptance and supports the concept of ordaining gay ministers. |
| Qualified acceptance | The organizational culture wishes to accept with certain conditions placed on the behavior (i.e., celibacy, not openly discussing it). |
| Absolute condemnation | The organizational culture rejects the behavior as amoral and will make no exception. |

Seven participants mentioned attempting heterosexual interaction of some sort. Some of these interactions were in high school, others college, and yet others later in life. Three participants were involved in a heterosexual marriage.

When asked about initial interaction with the gay culture, six participants provided pejorative elements in their responses. In this response, two participants questioned the definition of a gay culture. Conversely, the remaining six quickly identified specific elements of a culture.

As the participants provided their input to the interview questions, there are six themes that emerge in the process:

1. Don't Ask, Don't Tell

2. Local Supportive Organizational Cultures

3. Importance of Relational Leadership

4. Long-Term Relationship to the Organizational Culture

5. Empathy and Inclusiveness with Others

6. Sense of Duality Between the Organizational Culture and Psychosexual Development.

In discussing whether the organizational culture is supportive or nonsupportive, it is clear there were two themes that emerged. The first, being the organizational response from the hierarchy, which is described as a don't ask, don't tell policy. The second is a theme which emerges from their relationship to local congregations and colleagues which was often described as very supportive.

How do the individuals reconcile their belief structure as taught by the organizational culture in which they are immersed with their own developmental cycle of coming out? Their belief structures, as well as psychosocial development, develop with a strong sense of empathy and inclusiveness with others. There is a strong emphasis on their ability to relate to others.

Furthermore, there is a strong sense of duality that emerges between the organizational culture and their psychosexual development. The ministers need to reach outside the organizational culture to develop a healthy sense of self. Participants describe the need to be with other people who are like them.

What is the leader's reaction and interaction with the organizational culture during and after the coming out process? The leaders have a theme which develops focusing on relational leadership. Their ability to relate to others and emphasizing their honesty, integrity and achievement impacts their leadership development.

The second element of interaction focuses on the participant's long-term involvement in the organizational culture. The participant's reaction and interaction is marked by significant and long-term involvement, often from a very early age, with the organizational culture.

These themes were provided in this chapter to explain how the input was analyzed and how they begin to answer some of the research questions proposed in this study. In the next chapter, the researcher will discuss these themes in greater detail.

# 5

# *CONCLUSIONS AND RECOMMENDATIONS*

The research conducted here gathered the personal accounts of eight openly gay protestant clergy to examine their interaction with their organizational culture. This chapter shall present the conclusions and recommendations from the results. This chapter is organized into five sections: discussion, conclusions, application, limitations of the study, and recommendations for future research.

The discussion section shall contain an interactive discussion between the results and the current literature review. The findings of the study are paralleled to the research completed in previous studies. The discussion will present how the published research may or may not have been a predictor of the results of this study.

The conclusions section is a presentation of the conclusions one may draw from the discussion. Were the research questions answered by this study? This section will attempt to explain the conclusions that may be drawn from the discussion.

The application section provides recommendations for organizations based upon the discussion and conclusions. This section gives guidance to what organizations can do to develop more efficiently and deal with gay, male clergy in their organizational culture. As well, it provides pointers as what organizations may not want to do.

The limitations of the study section points out where the study founds its limitations. There were predestined limitations that were mentioned in the beginning of this study. As the study progressed, there are several limitations that were experienced. This section highlights those limitations.

The recommendations for future research provide researchers with suggestions on how to further this study. This section recommends how to take the current study to the next level and suggestions on how to check other theories this study brings up. The present study does not purport to be conclusive on the topic. This study simply means to open the discussion in the field for further research.

# Discussion

The discussion section shall review the six themes: don't ask, don't tell; local supportive organizational culture; importance of relational leadership; long-term relationship to the organizational culture; empathy and inclusiveness with others; and, sense of duality between the organizational culture and psychosexual development. This research contributes to the field of industrial and organizational psychology, in respect to, how employees (clergy) are developing within the organizational culture of the workplace (the church).

### Don't Ask, Don't Tell

A "Don't Ask, Don't Tell" policy describes a position by the organizations that it would not approve gay male clergy; however, they did not want to hear about whether the individual was gay or not. The majority of participants identified a clear nondisclosure policy from the organizational culture from the denominational position.

The binary system of coming out (Rasmussen, 2004) seems to be ruled, in the religious organizational culture explored here, by an unspoken nondisclosure policy. Participant 1 explained that, "I came to this church, which is my first church out of seminary, with my partner. Never publicly made a statement because I was told this is how we were supposed to do it." It is not as simple as being out or not. There is a way of doing things within the organizational culture of the church.

A policy of nondisclosure not only implies supervisors and denominational officials do not want to know, they wish for the development process to remain kept under wraps. They do not want to hear it from the clergy's congregations or fellow colleagues of the clergy. They may not even want to hear about it from the clergyperson themselves.

If individuals are in an organizational culture that does not support the coming out process (i.e., the don't ask, don't tell policy), then one can believe that overcoming the attitudes, behaviors, and beliefs that lead to discrimination will be more difficult to overcome on a corporate level of the organization. The organizational culture can simply see the gay clergy dynamic as an issue to be dealt with, rather than people who will have unexpressed needs.

The discrimination process is best dealt with by exposing to the individuals who facilitate the discriminatory process to those they discriminate against (Whitley & Kite, 2005). The reported position of the denominational persons prevents a personal exposure to the individual who is gay male minister. Therefore, denominational officials not only create a binary system as discussed by Rasmussen (2004); however, the organizational culture is created where the only way to gain success, maintain positive performance reviews, continue to receive appointments and so forth is to remain "in the closet."

One may assume that because the work environment may be described as discriminatory that the production level of gay clergy is lower than those of straight clergy. McNaught (1997) focused on explaining how the chief reason to rid organizations of discrimination is to increase the productivity of its workers. This is an issue that should be researched further (see Recommendations for Future Research in this chapter). However, clergy, as a compensating method, have learned to create supportive subcultures on the local level of their organization.

## Local Supportive Organizational Cultures

While the organizational culture of church superiors was not necessarily accepting, the local congregations and ministerial colleagues were found to be extremely supportive. Yip (2003) supported this conclusion as he explains that while the ministers have a negative experience with the church hierarchy, the local church is seen as much more supporting. There is a distinct difference in the local and hierarchical culture within the church.

Discrimination literature points out that the greatest way to overcome prejudice is to allow persons to know someone of the discriminated group personally (Whitley & Kite, 2005). It is always easier to maintain stereotyped perceptions, prejudicial attitudes, and discriminating behavior when it does not affect someone you really know. In these instances, the participants were becoming a face rather than an issue. People were not taking positions on the issue of homosexuality and their religion. They were taking positions on people they had come to know and trust, their pastor.

Finlay and Walther (2003) explained the strongest predictor of one's attitude on the issue of homosexuality is the individual's proximity to seeing a face rather than an issue. The clergy in this study describe the power of their relationships with individuals at the local level. One participant even discussed how local congregants knew before there was a disclosure to denominational persons. Several participants even identified support structures during the coming out process as individuals in their congregation. One participant relied on his local congregation to support him (even though he was not formally out) through his partner's death.

One area that may contribute to this is the constructs of occupational cultures (Dellinger, 2002) being met, even though the behavior was inconsistent with organizational culture. The occupational culture of ministry, which was not explored in this study, would place requirements of how a person should dress, look, act, and conduct oneself. It appears from the interviews that the participants functioned in their job with limited difficulty, except for their sexual orientation. This may contribute to the way the individuals were accepted locally. They looked like a minister. They talked like a minister. They dressed like a minister. They behaved like a minister. Therefore, they are the minister even if something was out of line with the organizational culture.

Another construct that may lend itself, in part or whole, to the development of a local accepting organizational culture is the view of ministers. Research shows that male ministers have feminine personality traits (Francis & Pearson, 1990; Robbins et al., 2001; Robbins et al., 1997). If one perceives gay men as having a stereotypical feminine behavior, then the reach to transferring the behavior as gay and clergy may not be that difficult.

Another construct that may lend itself to the dynamic may to be the "unplanned" development of an accepting local culture. Plant and Ryan (1988) claimed that an organizational culture can be planned to develop certain beliefs. Two themes that emerged in this study were the relational leadership and focus on empathy and inclusiveness. Do gay clergy, in an unplanned process, teach and implement the development of an accepting local organizational culture? This leads the discussion to the importance the relational leadership played in this.

## *Importance of Relational Leadership*

Relational leadership is the ability to lead through individual relationships that one develops over a period of time. Many may argue that relationships are simply a part of the leadership dynamic. In relational leadership, this study refers to the unique dynamic of relationships surpassing the boundaries that may exist in normal leadership models to become like an intimate family style.

The gay clergy in this study place an emphasis on their role as a leader and their relationship with those that they lead. These behaviors are often characterized by being someone the congregation can turn to, trust, and rely on. Significant emphasis was placed on their personal characteristics of making a real contribution, as being a good person, integrity, honesty and truth. The focus was on a strong following for more than just the role of a pastor. It appears the participants report their congregations liked them a great deal.

Lukenbill (1998) explained that one of the strongest elements in a gay and lesbian church's organizational culture is the relationships that are formulated. While this study is not supported in the typical mainline church, one can clearly see the leadership being developed through relationships. There is a strong reference in most statements about the individual's role as a leader of the church being directly connected to the connection with the people that surrounded this person and the relationship these people had with the leader.

Maxwell (2001) discussed how leadership needs to move from a positional point to one more focused on the relationship between the leader and the followers. The participants in this study explain that process through several examples. One participant's congregation discussed how they didn't know what to think about the whole gay thing; however, they didn't want to lose their leader. There was a connection and a bond that was formed through the relationships they developed with this person.

Perhaps, relational leadership is a part of the typical pastor. After all, being a minister is truly about having relationships with people. The focus on the occupational culture of clergy may have been developed in these individuals through long-term relationships with the church. Therefore, the discussion will follow to this long-term relationship.

## Long-Term Relationship to the Organizational Culture

The participants in this study enjoyed a long-term relationship with the organizational culture of their denomination. It was expected by the author that many persons would have changed denominations. In this study, only two persons changed denominations. Only one of those changes was directly associated with the fact he was gay.

All participants enjoyed a long, and seemingly positive, experience. Many of the participants went to church as a child, went through some form of catechism, vacation bible school, Sunday school, parochial schools, denominational colleges and seminaries. Individual participants even accounted for working in ministry focused work prior to their ordination. The super-imposed standards of behavior may have provided a structure for the coming out process.

The religious environment would have become a comfort zone. The church becomes a place where the individual learns how to navigate and become safe. The coming out process is marked with extreme stressors and maintaining a stable social status and environment may foster a healthier sense of development (Beaty, 1999; Coleman, 1982; Dube, 2000; Floyd & Stein, 2002; McFarland & McMahon, 1999; Newman & Muzzonigro, 1993).

Dube (2000) placed the awareness of sexual orientation at early teens. Yip (2003) explained the topic of homosexuality would be one the church would prefer to avoid. Therefore, while the individuals were dealing with the religiosity influence, the internalized homophobia that often appears during this time would be reinforced by unaccepting religious organizational cultures. This would have required the individuals to develop coping mechanisms to maintain a balance in their personal life through this period of time. One such coping mechanism may be their level of empathy and inclusiveness that is a markedly significant element in their ministry and personalities.

### Empathy and Inclusiveness with Others

Gay clergy show a significant level of empathy and inclusiveness for others. Their language is marked with terminology that indicates an awareness and acceptance of those they serve. They attribute this awareness directly to their coming out process.

During the developmental process of coming out they would have learned the discrimination process first hand. The discrimination that may have existed was overcome in the organizational culture by developing a local supportive culture, utilizing relational leadership, and experience from a long-term relationship with the organizational culture. These elements would also imply an increased awareness to marginalized persons.

Dube (2000) explained that younger individuals experiencing and navigating the coming out process successfully will develop an identity centered development. This identity centered personality may be more sensitive to the constructs of discrimination, marginalization, confusion, and pain. They may be more prone to being more empathic and accepting.

An important factor to remember here is that research (Francis & Pearson, 1990; Robbins et al., 2001; Robbins et al., 1997) shows that male clergy will be more likely to be more empathic. The question becomes if this behavior is influenced by their sexual orientation or clergy development. Perhaps, the reality is this behavioral development as a gay male makes them stronger candidates for the ministry.

### Sense of Duality between the Organizational Culture and Psychosexual Development

Finally, the last theme that emerged is their sense of duality. There is a duality between the organizational culture and the psychosexual development of the gay male clergy interviewed in this study. This dynamic can best be understood from the perspective of previous research.

The duality is formulated in the identity development process. Research shows that clergy often have an identity developed around the organizational culture of their church and their job, rather than the self (Kennedy et al., 1977). Other research (Beaty, 1999; Coleman, 1982; Dube, 2000; Floyd & Stein, 2002; McFarland & McMahon, 1999; Newman & Muzzonigro, 1993) explained that during the coming out process a sense of identity is developed.

Therefore, for the gay male clergy there are two distinct developmental processes occurring. One is that for the clergy and the other is that for the gay male. This comes through in their interviews as the individuals discuss their puritanical role of moral leader with behavior of the coming out process (i.e., exploration).

Many of the participants described a significant need to escape the church at times to maintain this duality. They talked about a need to associate with other individuals like they were. They mentioned having to connect with a gay culture. This was coupled with their need to maintain their identity with a religious organizational culture.

At the same time, several participants discussed their need to find a balance between their organizational culture and their psychosexual identity. Participants discussed their need to work through their homophobia and the homophobia of the church. It required them additional work in their coming out integration.

# Conclusions

The following are conclusions derived from the discussion and the research conducted in this study. These conclusions are applicable to the population studied within this research project. Further research studies should be conducted to gain any form of generalization of these conclusions.

Gay male clergy will gain an acceptance at a local level prior to being able to be accepted by their denomination. It is through the one on one contact that acceptance is garnered. This will occur at the local level where the clergy interact with people on a daily and weekly basis. Their contact is face to face.

It appears that the local organizational culture has a greater impact on the participants than the larger church culture did. Coleman (1982) explained that the level of impact a positive or negative reaction to the coming out process incurred is directly related to the value placed on the relationship. The participants placed more emphasis on gaining a supportive local organizational culture.

The level of support the organization as a whole offered was not a significant factor in the gay, male clergy development. Many of the organizational cultures were described as unsupportive. Other denominational cultures can simply be summed up with the adage of don't ask, don't tell. This was never a noteworthy point within the interviews. The clergy continued on to develop a local supportive culture.

Gay male clergy are on the front lines of battling the impending discrimination of the organizational culture of the church. They not only begin to set the tone of an organizational culture on the topic of homosexuality, the gay male clergy becomes the local face of the issue. Since research (Finlay & Walther, 2003; Whitley & Kite, 2005) showed the discrimination process is greatly impacted by exposure to someone from that group, one can clearly see why the gay, male clergy in the churches are leading the fight against that discrimination.

Gay male clergy present excellent people skills and are effective pastors. The participants of this study provided a strong focus on their interpersonal skills with their congregants. Gay male clergy may not show differing personality characteristics; however, they may show a heightened awareness to the situation. They have had to navigate these environments and become educated on working with people as they navigate their own coming out process.

The gay male clergy's focus on overcoming obstacles provided a strong sense of ingenuity and resourcefulness. They were required to learn street smarts of navigating the political paradigms of their denomination along with the book smarts of seminary. The participants each created a support network of supportive people, both in the seminaries and churches. They were able to navigate controversial issues in a politically and religiously charged environment.

This ability only sharpened their ability to create stronger relationships and make more effective leaders utilizing a relational leadership model. Their overt need for a support structure necessitates their ability to create this network at the very basic level of the organizational culture. Maxwell (2001) explained that people do not care how much you know until they know how much you care. The gay clergy in this study expressed a great deal of caring which allowed people to be open to following their leadership. The congregations followed the gay clergy's leadership even into counterdenominational teachings.

Organizations are always seeking to find the strengths and weaknesses of their employees. Effective organizations learn how to utilize those strengths and weaknesses to allocate their employees in the most efficient manner. Gay male clergy present a strong ability to work with marginalized groups of persons. Organizational leaders would be remiss not to identify the gay clergy's ability to understand the marginalized groups of persons in society and not only express sympathy, but truly express empathy. The development process of the gay clergy makes them ideal candidates to work with individuals who are in need of connection. The issue then becomes to examine the demographic of the denominations to determine how these skills could be utilized most effectively.

One thing that is needed for gay male clergy is the development of a healthy duality in which they are able to meet the needs of their personal identity from both a religious and a psychosexual realm. This can be accomplished through several means. Those means may include, but are not limited to, developing networks of gay clergy, publishing brochures to support clergy awareness, or providing additional social services for those clergy who may deal with the duality dynamic. Gay clergy need to have a safe and healthy outlet to experience the culture of who they are, as well as, be the minister they have trained to be.

# Limitations of the Study

Previously, the limitations of this study were provided for the reader. Those limitations primarily focused on the qualitative nature of the study. Those limitations included the quantitative perception of limitations steeped in focus, demographic of sample, hermeneutic of suspicion, and the lack of generalizability.

The focus of the study, while narrow, provided the first insight to the coming out process and the organizational culture of the church. When research is limited in a field, then an exploration of that field must be undertaken to develop further studies. This was accomplished in this research.

The demographics of the sample were expected to be a limitation. All participants are currently serving in the New York region. This limitation became minimized when it was discovered through the interviews that the participants moved here from several areas around the country. The participants moved to the New York region from states that included: Alaska, California, Florida, North Carolina, Ohio, and Texas. The sample was currently living in a limited demographic area; however, they represented a variety of origins.

The hermeneutic of suspicion is an excellent limitation that proved to be quite revelatory. There is no such thing as complete objectivity. One element the researcher realized in this process is the researcher's expectations of the results. The researcher expected to discover a much more pejorative and critical state of affairs for the participants. This proved to be untrue. The positive conclusions gave great insight to the learning process the research method allowed to come through.

This study does not purport generalizability. The study is a unique snapshot of the gay, male, Protestant clergy that became participants. The lived experience is their lived experience.

# Recommendations for Future Research

For future research, it is recommended to begin testing theoretical hypotheses this research presents. It is recommended that each of the conclusions be explored with further studies. One such conclusion may be referenced to the effectiveness of gay clergy versus the effectiveness of straight clergy. McNaught (1997) explained that discrimination in the workplace decreases effectiveness. Does a discriminatory work environment affect the effective work rate of gay male clergy?

Furthermore, it is recommended that a companion study be conducted utilizing female ministers. There is much research on female versus male ministers currently being published. It is recommended that research be conducted on whether lesbian ministers share similar experiences as the gay male ministers in this study.

It is also recommended that research be conducted in the dual identity development of gay ministers. How does this dual identity development affect the individual and the organizations? Is there anything the organizations can do to effectively assist in navigating this critical developmental process?

A study may be conducted utilizing a larger sample. This study may evaluate the conclusions of this study. This study may be effectively accomplished by utilizing a survey instead of interviews. This would allow a much larger sample to be evaluated with a larger diversity of demographics. A direction a larger study could take is to utilize quantitative measures.

Another study which may be conducted is one that diversifies the demographic of location. The gay male ministers in this study all came to the New York region; however, there are gay male ministers through out the United States. A study conducted in this manner would provide greater generalizability for the conclusions of this study.

Finally, it is important to acknowledge that this study was conducted utilizing gay male ministers who successfully came out and are serving as active clergy. It would be remiss to assume there are some who do not share a successful coming out process while maintaining their position as clergy. A study which would further investigate the coming out process in the organizational culture of the church would be to examine those who came out and could not maintain their role as clergy. What is the impact of the coming out process on that group of clergy and the impact the organizational culture had on them?

# References

Alas, R., & Vadi, M. (2003). The impact of organizational culture on organizational learning at six Estonian hospitals. *Trames: A Journal of the Humanities & Social Sciences, 7*(2), 83-99.

Allen, R. F., & Silverzweig, S. (1977). Changing community and organizational cultures. *Training & Development Journal, 31*(7), 28-35.

Bagraim, J. J. (2001). Organisational psychology and workplace control: The instrumentality of corporate culture. *South African Journal of Psychology, 31*(3), 43-50.

Beaty, L. A. (1999). Identity development of homosexual youth and parental and familial influences on the coming out process. *Adolescence, 34*(135), 597-601.

Boyle, M. A. (1997). Social barriers to successful reentry into mainstream organizational culture: Perceptions of people with disabilities. *Human Resource Development Quarterly, 8*(3), 259-268.

Browne, K. (2005). Snowball sampling: Using social networks to research non-heterosexual women. *International Journal of Social Research Methodology, 8*(1), 47-61.

Burns, R. W., & Cervero, R. M. (2004). Issues framing the politics of pastoral ministry practice. *Review of Religious Research, 45*(3), 235-254.

Cass, V. C. (1984). Homosexual identity formation: Testing a theoretical model. *The Journal of Sex Research, 20*(2), 143-167.

Celeste, B. L., Walsh, W. B., & Raote, R. G. (1995). Congruence and psychological adjustment for practicing male ministers. *The Career Development Quarterly, 43*(4), 374-384.

Chaffins, S., & Forbes, M. (1995). The glass ceiling: Are women where they should be? *Education, 115*(3), 380-387.

Chronicle, E. P., MacGregor, J. N., & Ormerod T. C. (2004). What makes an insight problem? The roles of heuristics, goal conception, and solution recoding in knowledge-learn problems. *Journal of Experimental Psychology: Learning, Memory, and Cognition, 30*(1), 14-27.

Clarke, V., Kitzinger, C., & Potter, J. (2004). "Kids are just cruel anyway": Lesbian and gay parents talk about homophobic bullying. *British Journal of Social Psychology, 43*, 531-550.

Cohen, R. C., & Swerdlik, M. E. (1999). *Psychological testing and assessment* (3rd ed.). Mountain View, CA: Mayfield.

Coleman, E. (1982). Developmental stages of the coming out process. *American Behavioral Scientist, 25*(4), 469-482.

Corrigan, P. W., & Matthews, A. K. (2003). Stigma and disclosure: Implications for coming out of the closet. *Journal of Mental Health, 12*(3), 235-248.

Croteau, J. M. (1996). Research on the work experiences of lesbian, gay, and bisexual people: An integrative review of methodology and findings. *Journal of Vocational Behavior, 48*, 195-209.

Darling, C. A., Hill, E. W., & McWey, L. M. (2004). Understanding stress and quality of life for clergy and clergy spouses. *Stress &*

*Health: Journal of the International Society for the Investigation of Stress, 20*(5), 261-277.

Dellinger, K. (2002). Wearing gender and sexuality "on your sleeve": Dress norms and the importance of occupational and organizational culture at work. *Gender Issues, 20*(1), 23-26.

Douglass, B. G., & Moustakas, C. (1985). Heuristic inquiry: The internal search to know. *Journal of Humanistic Psychology, 25*(3), 39-55.

Dube, E. M. (2000). The role of sexual behavior in the identification process of gay and bisexual males. *The Journal of Sex Research, 37*(2), 123-132.

Evangelical Lutheran Church. (2005). *Journey together faithfully: A call to study and dialogue.* Retrieved May 10, 2005, from http://elca.org/faithfuljourney/intro.html#more

Finke, R., & Dougherty, K. D. (2002). The effects of professional training: The social and religious capital acquired in seminaries. *Journal for the Scientific Study of Religion, 41*(1), 103-120.

Finlay, B., & Walther, C. S. (2003). The relation of religious affiliation, service attendance, and other factors to homophobic attitudes among university students. *Review of Religious Research, 44*(4), 370-393.

Floyd, F. J., & Stein, T. S. (2002). Sexual orientation identity formation among gay, lesbian, and bisexual youths: Multiple patterns of milestone experiences. *Journal of Research on Adolescence, 12*(2), 167-191.

Frame, M. W., & Shehan, C. L. (1994). Work and well-being in the two person career: Relocation stress and coping among clergy husbands and wives. *Family Relations, 43*(2), 196-205.

Francis, L. J. (2002). The personality characteristics of male Evangelical clergy: Denominational differences in the UK. *Mental Health, Religion, & Culture, 5*(2), 175-181.

Francis, L. J., & Pearson, P. R. (1990). Personality characteristics of mid-career male Anglican clergy. *Social Behavior & Personality, 18*(2), 347-400.

Francis, L. J., & Robbins, M. (2002). Psychological types of male Evangelical church leaders. *Journal of Beliefs and Values, 23*(2), 217-220.

Francis, L. J., & Thomas, T. H. (1997). Are charismatic ministers less stable? A study among male Anglican clergy. *Review of Religious Research, 39(1)*, 61-70.

Groves, P. A., & Ventura, L. A. (1983). The lesbian coming out process: Therapeutic concerns. *Personnel & Guidance Journal, 62*(3), 146-150.

Guess, J. B. (2005). *After twice rejecting UCC's ad, ABC airs "Focus on the Family" commercial.* Retrieved May 10, 2005, from http://www.ucc.org/news/r050305.htm

Hagestad, G. O., & Uhlenberg, P. (2005). The social separation of old and young: A root of ageism. *Journal of Social Issues, 61*(2), 343-360.

Herkelmann, K., & Dennison, T. (1993). Women in transition: Choices and conflicts. *Education, 114*(1), 127-144.

Hibbs, G. S. (2003). *The relationship challenge: Finding that special person and making it work.* New York: iUniverse.

Kennedy, E. C., Heckler, V. J., Kobler, F. J., & Walker, R. E. (1977). Clinical assessment of a profession: Roman Catholic clergymen. *Journal of Clinical Psychology, 33*(1), 120-128.

Kinman, R., & Kinman, G. (2000). "What's that got to do with making motor cars?" The influence of corporate culture on "in-company" degree programmes. *Journal of Education & Work, 13*(1), 5-24.

Kostere, K. (2004, October). *Research: Qualitative analysis II: Qualitative research models and data analysis.* Paper presented at the Capella University Colloquium Track 3, Landowne, VA.

Lahiry, S. (1994). Building commitment through organizational culture. *Training & Development, 48*(4), 50-53.

Lawson, R. B., & Ventriss, C. L. (1992). Organizational change: The role of organizational culture and organizational learning. *Psychological Record, 4* (2), 205-220.

Lee, C. (1999). Specifying intrusive demands and their outcomes in congregational ministry: A report on the ministry demands inventory. *Journal for the Scientific Study of Religion, 38*(4), 477-490.

Lukenbill, W. B. (1998). Observations on the corporate culture of a gay and lesbian congregation. *Journal for the Scientific Study of Religion, 37*(3), 440-453.

Malony, H. N., & Majovski, L. F. (1986). The role of psychological assessment in predicting ministerial effectiveness. *Review of Religious Research, 28*(1), 29-39.

Marszalek, J. F., III, & Cashwell, C. S. (1999). The gay and lesbian affirmative development model: Facilitating positive gay identity development. *Adultspan: Theory Research & Practice, 1*(1), 13-32.

Maxwell, J. (2001). *Developing the leader within you* (2nd ed.). Nashville, TN: Thomas Nelson.

McDonald, B. (2001). "Once you know something, you can't not know it": An empirical look at becoming a vegan. *Society & Animals, 8*(1), 1-22.

McFarland, W. P., & McMahon, T. R. (1999). Male archetypes as resources for homosexual identity development in gay men. *Journal of Humanistic Counseling, Education, & Development, 38*(1), 47-61.

McNaught, B. (1997). Making allies of co-workers: Educating the corporate world. In J. T. Sears & W. L. Williams (Eds.), *Overcoming heterosexism and homophobia: Strategies that work* (pp. 402-415). New York: Columbia University Press.

Molenaar, K., Brown, H., Caile, S., & Smith, R. (2002). Corporate culture. *Professional Safety, 47*(7), 18-28.

Moustakas, C. (1990). *Heuristic research: Design, methodology, and applications.* Thousand Oaks, CA: Sage.

Mulder, J. M. (1980). Ministry in America. In D. S. Schuller, M. P. Strommen, & M. L. Brekke (Eds.), *Ministry in America* (pp. 228-230). San Francisco: Harper and Row.

Nelsen, H. M., & Everett, R. F. (1976). Impact of church size on clergy role and career. *Review of Religious Research, 18*(1), 62-74.

Nelson, T. D. (2005). Ageism: Prejudice against our feared future self. *Journal of Social Issues, 61*(2), 207-221.

Newman, B. S., & Muzzonigro, P. G. (1993). The effects of traditional family values on the coming out process of gay male adolescents. *Adolescence, 28*(109), 213-227.

Olson, L. R., & Cadge, W. (2002). Talking about homosexuality: The views of mainline protestant clergy. *Journal for the Scientific Study of Religion, 41*(1), 153-167.

Patton, M. Q. (1997). *Utilization-focused evaluation: The new century text* (3rd ed.). Thousand Oaks, CA: Sage.

Patton, M. Q. (2002). *Qualitative research & evaluation methods* (3rd ed.). Thousand Oaks, CA: Sage.

Perl, P., & Chang, P. M. Y. (2000). Credentialism across creeds: Clergy education and stratification in Protestant denominations. *Journal for the Scientific Study of Religion, 39*(2), 171-188.

Perry, T. D., & Swicegood, T. L. P. (1990). *Don't be afraid anymore: The story of Reverend Troy D. Perry and the Metropolitan Community Churches.* New York: St. Martin's Press.

Plant, R., & Ryan, M. (1988). Managing your corporate culture. *Training & Development Journal, 42*(9), 61-66.

Priest, H. (2002). An approach to the phenomenological analysis of data. *Nurse Researcher, 10*(2), 50-64.

Rasmussen, M. L. (2004). The problem of coming out. *Theory into Practice, 43*(2), 144-150.

Raz, A. E. (1999). The hybridization of organizational culture in Tokyo Disneyland. *Studies in Cultures, Organizations & Societies, 5*(2), 235-264.

Robbins, M., Francis, L. J., Haley, J. M., & Kay, W. K. (2001). The personality characteristics of Methodist ministers: Feminine men and masculine women? *Journal for the Scientific Study of Religion, 40*(1), 123-129.

Robbins, M., Francis, L. J., & Rutledge, C. (1997). The personality characteristics of Anglican stipendiary parochial clergy: Gender differences revisited. *Personality and Individual Differences, 23*(2), 199-204.

Sarra, J., & Nakagashi, M. (2002). Balancing social and corporate culture in the global economy: The evolution of Japanese corporate structure and norms. *Law & Policy, 24*(4), 299-354.

Schein, E. H. (1986). What you need to know about organizational culture. *Training & Development Journal, 40*(1), 30-34.

Schein, E. H. (1993). Legitimating clinical research in the study of organizational culture. *Journal of Counseling & Development, 71*(6), 703-709.

Schermerhorn, J. R., Jr., Hunt, J. G., & Osborn, R. N. (2000). *Organizational behavior* (7th ed.). New York: John Wiley and Sons.

Schindler, P. (2004). Arson at office of L. I. gay flock. Retrieved May 11, 2005, from http://www.gaycitynews. com/gcn_338/arsonatofficeofli.html

Schneider, D. J. (2004). *The psychology of stereotyping.* New York: Guilford Press.

Sherkat, D. E. (2002). Sexuality and religious commitment in the United States: An empirical examination. *Journal for the Scientific Study of Religion, 41*(2), 313-323.

Singer, B. L. (1993). *Growing up gay/growing up lesbian: A literary anthology.* New York: The New Press.

Triandis, H. C., & Suh, E. M. (2002). Cultural influences on personality. *Annual Review of Psychology, 53*(1), 133-161.

Troiden, R. R. (1989). The formation of homosexual identities. *Journal of Homosexuality, 17*, 43-73.

Uy, J. M., Parsons, J. T., Bimbi, D. S., Koken, J. A., & Halkitis, P. N. (2004). Gay and bisexual male escorts who advertise on the Internet: Understanding reasons for and effects of involvement in commercial sex. *International Journal of Men's Health, 3*(1), 11-26.

Van Loon, M. (2003). The impact of fundamentalist Christian teaching on gay men. *Dissertation Abstracts International, 64* (5806), 64/11B. (UMI No. 3114107) Retrieved October 16, 2004, from http://wwwlib.umi.com/pqdd-pdf/ 7ed51671ff2049ab2c9d6887af9168b2/3996288

VanVianen, A. E. M., & Fischer, A. H. (2002). Illuminating the glass ceiling: The role of organizational culture preferences. *Journal of Occupational & Organizational Psychology, 75*(3), 315-337.

Waters, V. L. (2004). Cultivate corporate culture and diversity. *Nursing Management, 35*(1), 36-39.

Whitley, B. E., Jr., & Kite, M. E. (2005). *The psychology of prejudice and discrimination.* Belmont, CA: Thomson Higher Education.

Wilkinson, W. W., & Roys, A. C. (2005). The components of sexual orientation, religiosity, and heterosexuals' impressions of gay men and lesbians. *Journal of Social Psychology, 145*(1), 65-83.

Yip, A. K. T. (2003). Spirituality and sexuality: An exploration of the religious beliefs of non-heterosexual Christians in Great Britain. *Theology & Sexuality: The Journal of the Institute for the Study of Christianity & Sexuality, 9*(2), 137-155.

# APPENDIX A

## *TELEPHONE SCRIPT TO RECRUIT PARTICIPANTS*

Journey of the Sacred Leader:
A Heuristic Inquiry Examining the Coming Out Process in the Corporate Culture of a Religious Setting for Gay, Male, Protestant Clergy

Hello _____,

My name is Shane Hibbs. I am a doctoral student in the Organizational Psychology program at Capella University and I am preparing to conduct research for my dissertation. I am a gay protestant minister and my dissertation research examines the coming out process in a religious organizational culture for gay, male, protestant clergy.

I am calling you because you are an openly self-identified gay minister. I would like to send you a sheet to give you basic information on the study and request your participation. Would you be willing to look over a brief introduction to my research and consider participating?

### If the prospective participant responds in the affirmative

Thank you so much. I will mail this sheet to you and will follow up with you within 5 business days. After you have looked over the introduction then we will set up a time to meet so we can go over the consent form if you wish to proceed. Once again, thank you so much for your time. I will look forward to speaking with you more. Have a good day.

### If the prospective participant responds in the negative

Thank you so much for your time. I appreciate your time. Have a good day.

# APPENDIX B

## *STUDY INFORMATION SHEET*

Journey of the Sacred Leader:
A Heuristic Inquiry Examining the Coming Out Process in the Corporate Culture of a Religious Setting for Gay, Male, Protestant Clergy

You are being asked to participate in a research project by G. Shane Hibbs, a doctoral student with Capella University School of Psychology, for the purpose of examining the coming out process in the corporate culture of a religious setting for gay, male, Protestant clergy.

In order to participate you must:

1. Be 21 years of age or older

2. Be an Openly Gay Male

3. Be an Ordained Protestant Minister

4. Sign an Informed Consent Form

You do not have to be currently serving a congregation/parish.

This study will examine:

1. The Coming Out Process

2.  Religious Organizational Culture

3.  Clergy Development

Your participation will consist of one interview which will be transcribed, and you will be given a follow up opportunity to add any clarification or additional information to your interview. All participation is strictly voluntary (no compensation is provided) and all information gathered is confidential. All participants' identification is anonymous.

As a way to keep all participants informed of the outcomes of this research, each participant will be given a copy of the completed dissertation, after its approval from Capella University.

If you have any questions you may contact:

Researcher: G. Shane Hibbs
            [address and phone number omitted]

Research Supervisor: Dr. Wayland Secrest
                     (wayland.secrest@capella.edu)
                     Capella University
                     225 South 6th Street, 9th Floor
                     Minneapolis, MN 55402
                     1-888-227-3552

# APPENDIX C
## *INFORMED CONSENT*
## *FORM*

 CAPELLA UNIVERSITY

225 South 6th Street, 9th Floor
Minneapolis, MN 55402

I, _____, agree to participate in a research study for the purpose of examining the lived experience of the coming out process for gay, male, Protestant clergy in the organizational culture of the Church. The duration of this study will be for one (1) year with my participation lasting for the length of the interviews and follow-up. It is not expected that my participation will exceed five (5) hours. My participation is voluntary and I have the right to withdraw from this process at any time by simply notifying the researcher of my desire to no longer participate. There will be no consequences for withdrawing from the study

The data being collected is being utilized for the Dissertation Research, entitled Journey of the Sacred Leader: *A Heuristic Inquiry Examining the Coming Out Process in the Corporate Culture of a Religious Setting for Gay, Male, Protestant Clergy*, of G. Shane Hibbs, a doctoral student, in his pursuit of a Ph.D. in Psychology. There are eight (8) participants in this study, including myself. I was selected because I met the criteria of the research sample (Gay, Male, Protestant, Ordained Clergy), and I was known to the researcher or referred to the researcher. The information can be utilized for the dissertation and any other future publications based upon this research.

I understand that I will be participating in standardized face to face interview with the researcher. I will receive a copy of the interview questions no later than 48 hours prior to the scheduled interview date. The interview will take place in my home or office, whichever is more comfortable for me.

I understand the only risk to this research is that I may experience strong emotions during the interview process and follow-up. I have the right to stop my participation in the research being conducted at any time. Furthermore, I understand there is no compensation being offered for my participation. However, the benefit of this process is that I will get to participate in contributing to the field of research that is attempting to help others who are dealing with similar issues and I will be informed of significant new findings by receiving a copy of the dissertation upon its completion.

I have been advised that my participation in research on a sensitive topic is taken seriously. Confidentiality is of great importance to foster a safe and secure environment where I am able to open up and disclose comfortably. Therefore, my name and identifying data will be not be published. The personal data that will be published will not identify the interviewee data (i.e., age and denomination) together, and furthermore, each individual will be assigned a number and the study will only refer to the subject number. These steps are put in place to maintain anonymity of the subjects.

I further understand that my interview will be audio taped with two recording devices. One of those tapes will be secured in a Bank Security Vault and the other will be sent to a professional confidential transcriptionist. The audio tape and transcripts of the interview will then be sent back to the researcher by certified U.S. mail. Then I will receive a copy of my interview transcript and will have the opportunity to provide a written statement of any additional data that I wish to include.

All hard copies of the interviews will be kept secured in a locked safe, when not in use, in order to ensure the data is kept confidential.

If at any time there is a question about my rights, the research study, or for research-related injury then I may contact:

Researcher: G. Shane Hibbs
    [address and phone number omitted]

Research Supervisor: Dr. Wayland Secrest
    (wayland.secrest@capella.edu)
    Capella University
    225 South 6th Street, 9th Floor
    Minneapolis, MN 55402
    1-888-227-3552

Internal Review Board Supervisor: Dr. Karen Yasgoor
    (karen.yasgoor@capella.edu)
    Capella University
    225 South 6th Street, 9th Floor
    Minneapolis, MN 55402
    1-888-227-3552

I have read the consent form in its entirety and understand it completely. I have received a copy of this consent form. I further attest that any questions regarding this study have been answered satisfactorily. Furthermore, I consent to be a part of this research until such time that I withdraw.

Name of Participant (Please Print): _____

Signature of Participant: _____

Date of Signature: _____

# APPENDIX D

## *INTERVIEW QUESTIONS*

1. What is your name and date of birth?

2. At what age were you ordained?

3. What denomination were you ordained in?

4. What denomination are you currently active in, if any? If you are not active, why not?

5. If you are active in a denomination, then what is your role in the denomination you are currently active in?

6. At what age did you come out?

7. When you came out, were you in high school, college, seminary, or serving in a parish/church?

8. Describe the organizational culture that existed in your denomination on the issue of homosexuality.

9. Describe how representatives of your denomination found out about your sexual orientation.

10. Tell me about life before you came out?

11. Describe the relationship between the church and yourself before you came out?

12. What was it like when you first experienced the gay culture?

13. Describe the most memorable "first" that you experienced as a gay male.

14. While experiencing this first, can you recall any imagery, thoughts, or feelings you experienced about your church?

15. Tell me about your coming out experience.

16. Describe how a denominational leader reacted when you came out.

17. Describe how your peers (either fellow seminary students or clergy) reacted when you came out.

18. Describe how the laity reacted when you came out.

19. Have any of these persons' reactions changed over time and if so how?

20. How do you reconcile, as a religious leader, the organizational culture of your denomination and your sexual orientation?

21. How has accepting your own sexual orientation affected your development as a religious leader?

# Appendix E

## *INTERVIEW QUESTIONS REVIEW*

Journey of the Sacred Leader:
A Heuristic Inquiry Examining the Coming Out Process in the Corporate Culture of a Religious Setting for Gay, Male, Protestant Clergy

Interview Questions Review

You are being asked to evaluate the interview questions for a research project which is being conducted by Mr. G. Shane Hibbs in partial fulfillment of his Doctor of Philosophy degree in Psychology with Capella University. You are being asked to read the Dissertation Prospectus and answer the following questions. Please do not put your name on this document anywhere. Your honesty is much appreciated.

Reviewer is ☐ Mental Health Practitioner
☐ Active Clergy
☐ Open and Identified Gay

1. Do you feel the questions will provide answers that the research claims to be examining?

2. Are the questions open and do not attempt to lead the participants to specific conclusions?

3. Do you feel they are in appropriate order? If not, why?

4. Do you feel the questions are worded correctly?

   A. Would you change the wording on any?

   B. Which one(s) and how?

5. Do you have any additional feedback you would like to provide?

Please write down all your comments and submit this form along with the draft of the prospectus back to Mr. G. Shane Hibbs.

978-0-595-40035-5
0-595-40035-3